DANCE OF THE CHAMELEON

A VIETNAM MEDIC'S STORY

BY

JAMES R. SQUADRITO

with

ARLENE VIOLET

PAGE PUBLISHING, INC.
New York, NY

First originally published by Page Publishing, Inc. 2015

ISBN 978-1-68213-200-5 (pbk)
ISBN 978-1-68213-201-2 (digital)

Printed in the United States of America

I dedicate this book to my dad, J.T. Squadrito, who served his country faithfully as a Combat Medic during World War II; and to my mom Helen who cared and kept our family together during the ups and downs of life.

I would also dedicate this book to the millions of men and women who served, fought, and gave their lives to defend our freedom.

I thank Michele, my wife, my love, my best friend, my confidant who has kept me going all these years; and my children Chantele and Daniel who have supported me with patience and understanding.

Finally, I thank God for giving me the time to finish this project that I hope someday will inspire others to leave a legacy for those who might follow.

My Dad and I in dress Army Medic Uniforms.

HERO

I thought I was a hero
'Cause people told me so.
The crowd would cheer me on
I shined from head to toe.

My life was filled with parties
All night and through the day.
I had my choice of ladies
They all came my way.

Chorus
Hero, hero, walking proud and strong
Hero, hero, where do you belong?

Somewhere across the ocean
A war was raging on
I heard from Richard Nixon
You're joining us in 'Nam.

They trained me as a medic
And sent me to the front.

There we met the Vietcong
And we were on the hunt.

Chorus
Hero, hero, walking proud and strong
Hero, hero, where do you belong?

I tended to the wounded
And watched as others died.
My aching heart was hardened
The government had lied.

But though all these horrors
I managed to survive.
Remembering my lost friends
Until the day I die.

Chorus
Hero, hero, walking proud and strong
Hero, hero, where do you belong?
Where do you belong?

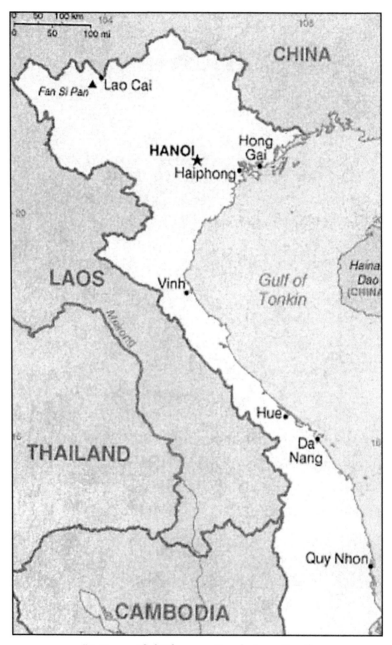

"A Beautiful Place to Look At—But"
As a college student, I never knew where Vietnam was or cared
until I saw it on TV. I would soon know too much about it.

PREFACE

Cha-me-leon. A person given to often expedient or fac-
ile change in ideas or character sometimes in order to
please people or to succeed.(*Merriam Webster*)

I wrote the main part of this book forty-two years ago after I had been
home from Vietnam a short while. I wrote it primarily as a catharsis. I
had tried my very best in Vietnam to be the kind of soldier who would
make my country and my family proud. You will see my failings in that
regard.

Our brothers and sisters back in the states largely hated us when we
all returned. Their hatred was no match for the self-loathing many of us
had for ourselves. All war is ugly, and this one lived up to that reputation.
I met some soldiers and people who act heroically. Many more, however,
were grunts just like me, and we did not act as honorably as we should
have. We may have been honorably discharged, but that was just about it
as far as honor was concerned.

It wasn't from a lack of trying. The culture of this war—sex, dope,
and rock and roll—influenced our conduct in ways I wished it hadn't. As
a medic out in the field and having served in three locations in Vietnam
during that war, I was sometimes just as scared by my troops who were
high on drugs as much as I was of the Vietcong bullets and mortars shot
into the battleground. The black-white fight of the civil rights movement back in the states in 1969 was in full swing on the battlefield in
Southeast Asia. I considered it fratricide when any black soldier came

into the aid support station with a bullet from an American gun, not that of the Vietcong. Some African American soldiers gave it as good as they got.

Our behavior toward the Vietnamese women left a lot to be desired. We rationalized sexual activity with very young girls. Had we done this in the states, some soldiers would have been convicted of statutory rape.

Looking back at my earlier life, I was a chameleon. I really needed to make people like me and would act and react in ways to curry favor that make me cringe now.

I was a mess when I returned back to Rhode Island. I was depressed and nearly suicidal. I couldn't hold down a job as I plowed through twelve or more job opportunities. Then redemption came slowly but surely and painfully. Eventually, I became an executive of a *Fortune 500* company.

So I wrote this book as an expiation but also with the hope that soldiers who came back psychically scarred can read about my failures and gain encouragement that all is not lost for our characters. We can make it. There's a lot to be proud of. There's an inner reserve we can tap.

I am a member of the medics who came before me and after me. Their motto, "A medic is never so tall as when he stoops down to aid a soldier," sticks with me.

Never a day goes by that the war doesn't crowd my thoughts during the day or in my nightmares. But I have learned to live with the medic's motto more than the nightmares. I pray that the same will be said of my comrades in arms in any unit as we help one another to recover from our battle scars.

There are 1,354 combat medics, who died while trying to save their men, listed on the Vietnam memorial. This is a story of one of them who lived to tell it.

James R. Squadrito

CHAPTER 1

THE RIGHT STUFF?

"Kill me!"

I wasn't sure I understood his whisper, so I bent my head lower. I looked at him, and there was no mistake even before he spoke again. His brown eyes were pleading with me to end his life.

"Kill me. I can't let my fiancée see me like this."

"This" was a torso of a once strapping, handsome twenty-two-year-old soldier. His arms and legs were blown off after he stepped on a Claymore mine in Lai Khe. The insidiousness of this hidden weapon was that it blew straight up once a soldier activated it. Sp5c. John Marshall was the first victim of a land mine that I had seen as a newly minted medic in my first three weeks of assignment.

I felt myself recoil at the sight of this poor guy. I wretched but tried to cover my reaction like I was stifling a cough.

"Buddy, we're going to take good care of you." I was conning myself as well as him.

I flashed back to when I was eight years old. I was riding a school bus home from South Bellingham elementary school when it swung onto Main Street to pick up my school chum, nine-year-old Chad Marco. Chad had the status of the cool patrol boy at his school, North Bellingham Elementary. I waved out the window, and he saluted back with his right hand. His left arm was outstretched to act as a block to the students queued up behind him, including his sister, Maria, who was three kids back. All of a sudden, I saw Chad slip. The bus bumped upward, and I heard screams outside. The somewhat elderly bus driver put the bus in reverse, and the bus went bump again. I shot out of my seat and opened the door. There was Chad under the wheels with his arms and legs all akimbo, his very life crushed out of him.

I felt tears running down my cheeks and wiped them away. I wasn't sure for whom I was crying.

"Do it! I'm begging you." The soldier's voice brought me back to the present. I frantically looked around for a doctor to tend to him. I didn't have much hope. We used an ABCDE system to describe the soldiers' conditions. Priority was given to those who could be saved. Specialist Marshall was in the lowest category.

I struggled with his request. On the one hand, I thought he'd probably die anyway, so what was the harm in putting him out of his misery. Yet snuffing out a life was counter to everything I had been trained to do. Medics save lives; we don't take them. My Catholic upbringing also trumped my thoughts. God alone should decide when somebody gets called to heaven from this hell on earth.

While I was doing the equivalent of arguing how many angels fit on the head of a pin, Specialist Marshall decided the issue for me. He sighed and expired.

I was numb. I wiped my eyes with the top of my tee shirt and looked around for a sheet or blanket to cover my comrade.

I was forever changed from that day on. I came into the Vietnam War as a somewhat spoiled boy. I grew up to be a man at that very moment in the support aid unit.

CHAPTER 2
THE BEGINNING

When the chopper first came in with Specialist Marshall, it was 1640 hours. I wasn't hungry, so I went back to my hooch. Fortunately, my roommate was at the mess hall. I threw myself down on my bunk and began to think about how I had gotten myself into this war. I was so stupid. All of my fraternity brothers at the then Bryant College(now a university) knew enough to sign up for the National Guard back in the days when the soldiers weren't deployed much, if at all.

I should have been more attentive to Richard Milhous Nixon's intonations about the growing conflict in Southeast Asia. Since the events leading up to and during the war weren't on the sport pages, I paid little attention to world events. Instead, I was busy developing my reputation as a jock and a party animal. My fraternity, Theta Chi, was nicknamed The Animals, and we brothers all worked hard to be worthy of the title. I harder than most. Right then, I was feeling pretty embarrassed that I had been such a gadfly.

I couldn't believe that just a short time ago, I was caught up with kid's stuff like eating a veritable menagerie of goldfish, lizards, frogs, spiders, and occasional road kill during pledge week. One night, the frat boys locked me up in a room with forty-five puppies that were given Ex-Lax, and they kept me there naked and tied up. The room and I were loaded with pup poop, and I had to return to class on Monday with only a thimbleful of water with which to wash. The professor dismissed the class after five minutes for some unknown reason.

Completing my ignominy was my tie-up at an Indian reservation in Fall River, Massachusetts. The temperature dipped to 15 degrees overnight, and I was given a Mohawk haircut, colored red. I had a basketball game the next evening, and the coach nearly benched me until four other teammates strolled in with similar tonsorial splendor in a show of solidarity. My older sister Carol bought me my first car after pledging, which I totaled a week later.

I was dumb enough to brag that I only had one notebook for all my classes for four years. As my popularity rose off and on the court, my grades headed in the opposite direction. The professors weren't going to put up with me just because I could make a jump shot. I flunked two courses, so I had to be fifth year student. The trouble I didn't foresee was that, in 1969, you had to be in school full time to avoid the draft. Now Uncle Sam had me by the cojones.

I tried to solve my dilemma. My parish pastor, Father Germani, had successfully written letters to get some parish boys who were drafted to serve stateside. I was certain that I could charm a letter out of him. My father and I waited for him in the parlor of the rectory. He brought in a ledger book and nodded his head in a way that I didn't like.

"No," he told us. "You only contributed $52 dollars during the last twelve months in the collection plate. Not enough for a letter. The minimum is $100."

My father offered to supplement the amount within three weeks, but somehow, the priest thought that would be unethical. The pastor offered to keep me in his prayers as we quit the place. In silence, we drove back home to break the news to my mother. My father was still puzzled as to why I had been drafted since I was supposedly a master's degree candidate. I was a coward and hadn't told my parents that I'd fallen short of undergrad credits.

In the spring, the invitations to my graduation party had gone out, so I figured I'd go through the celebration and tell them afterward at an appropriate time. The party turned into a Cecil B. DeMille movie with so many guests that I didn't recognize everybody. At the bash, I felt like a fraud, accepting gifts from the relatives. Many a slap on the back accompanied the sentiment of pride that I was the first family member to have a college degree. Several times, I thought about coming clean then and there about my failure but chickened out.

In fact, I felt like chicken shit when my father brought up my grandfather, who had bought a ticket for his brother to come to America for the dream. He wept as he told the story again about how this brother perished in steerage on the *Titanic*. Looking around the room, my older relatives were all crying as though they were hearing the story for the first time.

Then my father hoisted a glass. He began by recounting his own father's barbershop success in a small village outside of Palermo, Sicily, until the Black Hand mobsters came looking for a weekly "donation" for protection. With a tear falling on his shirt as he looked heavenward, he thanked his father for bringing his family of ten children and wife to the land of the free and the home of the brave.

I was a bit taken back by this show of affection since my father previously told me that my grandfather drowned himself in a sea of booze after losing his brother on the *Titanic*. He often had abused his wife, my grandmother Camilla, who died in her early forties from fatigue and domestic violence. In fact, my father took to protecting his brothers and sisters from his old man.

My dad became a Golden Gloves boxing phenomenon by age eighteen with aspirations of becoming a world champ. His dream died after a bar fight beating he gave a kid. His hands were registered weapons as a professional fighter. He was subsequently banned from the sport. He worked as a foundry worker thereafter to provide for us kids and my mother Helen with regret, no doubt, as to what could have been. I was mortified as my father turned toward me with a final salute, "Son, you did your family proud!" Cheers of "Chin chi" echoed all around me.

A few days later, my father found out quite by accident about my academic status. On the back of his car was a Bryant College bumper sticker which, in retrospect, I wish I hadn't given him. While he was filling up his tank, another vehicle driven by Academic Dean Robert Smith pulled into the filling station. Noticing the sticker, the dean asked if he had somebody attending the college. My father proudly told him that his son had graduated just a few days before.

"What's his name?"

"James Squadrito."

The dean paused then spilled the beans that I hadn't finished my course work.

When my father confronted me, I felt lower than snake spit. I sent all the money given to me as a graduation gift back to my family members with a letter of explanation. At least I had my girlfriend, or so she told me.

I decided to embrace my new career. On one level, I was happy that I was drafted since it gave me the chance to prove to my father that I was a stand-up guy. At the Pawtucket, Rhode Island, recruitment center, I saw my fellow inductees mimicking homosexual behavior, so they'd be coughed out of the system. Guys limped in with conjured up injuries and supporting documentation from family friendly doctors. I wasn't tempted to play either role since my humiliation required penance. I would face the music.

Lying on the bunk, I felt that I screwed up my life though. My dad had made a fatal error at age eighteen, which ended his career. I had four years on him, and I managed to mess up my life.

I was going to make the best of it. I resolved again, I was going to make him proud of me.

"Send These Boys to Camp"
In 1967 a little college in RI called Bryant brought together fraternity
brothers from Theta Chi Fraternity who played basketball and compiled
a 23-0 record. Since then the school is now a university and is playing
a division 1 schedule. I am very proud of our accomplishments
in my # 30 uniform. Years later the team, including myself was
inducted into the Bryant University Athletic Hall of Fame.

"Coming to the Land of Plenty"
My Grandma & Grandpa Squadrito came to America
to escape persecution in Sicily. These are 5 of their 10
children who were brought up in tough times in Pawtucket,
RI. Notice the great smile on Grandpa's face!!!

CHAPTER 3

LICENSE TO KILL

With my roommate still chowing down, I continued to evaluate my performance with Specialist Marshall and my army experience to date. There actually wasn't too much to review. I performed like a mope. So far my time in this man's army had been anything but salutary, starting with boot camp.

Twenty-two weeks earlier, I had traveled from the Pawtucket, Rhode Island, center to Ft. Dix, New Jersey, for boot camp. I never heard so many guys be so quiet. I was just as glad because I wanted to keep my own counsel. Looking around, I sized up the other saps that were going to hell with me. Most of them were younger and seemed more poorly dressed. I also never saw so many minorities in one place. My private education had been pretty segregated.

Sergeant Stoico was waiting for us on the other end. He was a black belt karate pro from Japan. All muscle at 5'8", he was nobody with whom to tangle. He commenced his humiliation of us immediately. Our first stop was at the barbers where we got our hair trimmed to a stubble. He had records on all of us. He made me a platoon leader, I think, because of my college education. My job was to make sure that everybody was on time and to march the company to and from exercises.

We were all hauled into an auditorium for orientation. They're must have been at least five thousand guys. A uniform asked if anybody could entertain. When nobody raised a hand, I shot up and said yes. I went on the stage and belted out Tennessee Ernie Ford's "Big Bad John." The place went wild.

The next morning, when I was washing dishes on KP (kitchen patrol), a major came into the kitchen and asked me to follow him into an office just outside. "What the hell did I do?" I wondered as he told me to be seated in front of him. He pulled out some paperwork.

"I see you used to be an entertainer in your previous life."

I told him that I had put together some musical shows in college and had done some singing around town.

"I heard you sing 'Big Bad John.' Pretty good job." He went on to tell me that the general's wife was having a birthday party, and he was putting on a show to celebrate her day. The deal was that if I agreed to sing at the bash, I would have no more KP.

This was a no-brainer, and I said yes.

The general's wife's favorite song was "I Left My Heart in San Francisco," and I was assigned that song to sing. It was the best performance I had ever done, and I received a standing ovation for giving the wife her wish to hear Tony B's megahit from her hometown. I was having a ball and rubbing elbows with the elite officers in the camp during rehearsals instead of peeling spuds and getting dishpan hands.

The next day, I was summoned to my barracks to the officer's club. En route, I was running through a song list that I could sing to dazzle everyone. The major and three other officers met me at the club.

"We got great news for you. This is your lucky day. There is an opening at the club for an entertainer."

The person would be in charge of all the shows at the club and would spend his tour of duty right there at Ft. Dix. I went bug-eyed. The major added a little caveat that it was between me and another recruit but he liked me better. The frosting on the cake would be that I'd be promoted to private first class (PFC). I was elated. Walking back to the barracks, I was planning shows. A little nagging sensation ate at me as I wondered who my competition was. Yet I remained confident that he could not have pulled off the performance I'd done for the general's wife. I figured she must have some pull! I was sure the post was locked up.

I was called from the shooting range the next day and driven to the officer's club. I could feel a slight chill in the room when I saw the major's face. He started by reiterating that I was his favorite entertainer and that when I got discharged, I should pursue a career in entertainment. Unfortunately, he announced, the other guy got chosen for the job over me.

Thanking him, I dragged myself back to peeling potatoes. At the end of my boot camp, I asked the major who the guy was who beat me out of the job.

"Frank Sinatra Jr."

Had daddy made a phone call? I never was sure whether Frank Jr. was recruited or just selected to entertain the troops in order to launch his career.

Meanwhile, my luck was running poorly. Very shortly after getting nixed for the entertainment job duties, I got fired from being the platoon leader. I was marching my troops with unorthodox boogie-woogie steps one day when a senior officer spotted us. I was quickly relieved of my post.

From one day to another, we never knew what time we would get up. Five a.m. was late. Many times we'd be awakening at 3:00 a.m. or 4:00 a.m. for a March or double-time run. Sargent Stoico often made me and other guys who were the most athletic do fifty pushups or a dying cockroach crawl. I thought he wanted the others to see us winded, so they'd be worried about how they would fare when their time came to crawl through mud.

After ten minutes to get dressed, we marched to mess hall and had eight–ten minutes to eat the swill that passed for food. Day after day we had powdered eggs and toast. Lunch wasn't much better with some cream chicken slop served practically every other day. Usually at night, we had time to ourselves after dinner.

Classes were interesting. I loved learning how to pull apart and put together my M16 rifle. Driving my bayonet into a dummy was particularly gratifying since it got my aggressions out. God forgive me, but I even imagined that I was gutting Monsignor Germani.

Reconnaissance classes taught us how to look for trip wires and how to be the point man, that is, the person who went ahead to scout the enemy. I was pretty good getting through the mazes. Live ammo was fired over our heads, so I became adept at the belly crawl. I must confess that I really didn't pay too much attention to survival skills since I was convinced that I'd get a clerk's job because of my education and land someplace in Hawaii or Guam instead of Vietnam. I often lobbied the brass to secure such a position.

Being competitive, I wanted to win the Universal Soldier awards, not only because I wanted to be considered a topnotch solider, but also because that was a way to get a liberty pass. But I cheated.

I paid guys a couple of bucks each week to make my bunk since I didn't know how to make it so tight that a quarter would bounce on it. I never saw any sense to doing this either since we'd probably be sleeping eventually on mats in a jungle. I also paid weekly to have my shoes and my brass polished. Twenty bucks bought my expert marksmanship medal from the gunnery officer in charge. Later on, this honor would backfire since I would be selected as a point man because of my alleged way with a firearm. All I was thinking of then though was getting a pass to get off the base.

Both on the base as well as when I was on liberty I began to notice tensions between black and white soldiers. In the mid- to late '60s civil rights was just percolating. There was a lot of prejudice expressed by white guys during conversations. During liberty, I witnessed some vicious fights between whites and black soldiers. One-on-one beatings weren't as bad as they were with five or six guys each fighting each other. The MPs were constantly breaking up fights. Later, I would see much worse in combat, including murders of black soldiers. White soldiers were also killed by black troops.

When we got a pass to go into town, I was pretty tame. Maybe I was maturing. I'd frequent a bar where I saw Junior Walker and the All Stars perform. While I could have stayed overnight in the town, I would return back to the barracks. I met a GI from Central Falls, Rhode Island, and he took pity on me. He had his girlfriend bring up a date for me. She was more of a friend who was seeking to have a pen pal. I was still hearing from my college girlfriend although her correspondence grew less and less. I didn't want to be a jerk and cheat on her, at least not so soon.

After two weeks, I was encouraged by the platoon clerk to think about becoming an officer and attending Officer Candidate School (OCS). I didn't want to do this for a couple of reasons. One, I wanted to get out of the service as fast as possible and didn't want the extra time that would be required to serve. I also had been warned of the dislike that the rank and file had for officers. Rumors were rampant that some officers had been killed by friendly fire because they were regarded as officious by the rank and file who were drugged out of their minds during battle. I deliberately flunked the exam. I didn't like the odds.

Much later when I was in the DMZ (demilitarized zone), I thanked my old friend, John Powers, who had already served a tour in Vietnam and who warned me that second Louies (second lieutenants) were an endangered species. Their life expectancy was about three months in 'Nam either because the North Vietnamese soldier got a bonus of $15 for bagging an officer or the second Louie was body bagged because of friendly fire. My job later in the field would prove him right. One of the most horrendous stories involved the death of Second Lieutenant Donald Peterson, which I will discuss later.

At the end of the six-week training, thousands of us were waiting for our MOS (military occupational specialty) that would signify what we'd be turned into and where we were off to next.

"Listen for your name," the major shouted as the thousands of us stood in the open field.

"Squadrito 91 Bravo" was what I heard. I was thinking about sitting some place sweet, filling out reports as a company clerk. The guys on either side of me gave me condolences as 91 Bravo, they explained, was the worst MOS you could get since it meant combat medic, and in 'Nam there was no honoring the Geneva Convention governing the war where medics were supposed to be protected. A medic not only had to take care of all the wounded but also had to fight to save his ass as well.

There was a huge shortage of medics because they were a huge target for the Vietcong forces. The communist government paid a bounty if certain platoon members were killed. Fifty dollars if they got a radio operator because the troops would have no contact with the rear or a means to contact 'copters to evacuate the wounded, $25 for the medic because morale would be severely damaged by his demise, and $15 for an officer in charge because that would leave the soldiers with no leader to get back safely.

I could only imagine what hell was in store for me as I said good-bye to friends I would probably never see again.

Now as I ruminated in my hooch, I thought that I had visited hell with the arrival of Specialist Marshall. I tried to shake off the image of his missing limbs.

SELECTIVE SERVICE SYSTEM

Approval Not Required.

ORDER TO REPORT FOR INDUCTION

RHODE ISLAND
LOCAL BOARD NO. 5
RM. 202, POST OFFICE BLDG.
PAWTUCKET, R. I. 02860

(LOCAL BOARD STAMP)

The President of the United States,

To   James R. Squadrito
936 Main Ave.
Warwick, R. I. 02886

June 1, 1969
(Date of mailing)

SELECTIVE SERVICE NO.			
37	5	46	574

GREETING:

You are hereby ordered for induction into the Armed Forces of the United States, and to report

at   Room 202, Post Office Bldg., Pawtucket, R. I.
(Place of reporting)

on   July 1, 1969   at   7:00 A.M. sharp.
(Date)   (Hour)

for forwarding to an Armed Forces Induction Station.

(Member or clerk of Local Board)

IMPORTANT NOTICE
(Read Each Paragraph Carefully)

IF YOU HAVE HAD PREVIOUS MILITARY SERVICE, OR ARE NOW A MEMBER OF THE NATIONAL GUARD OR A RESERVE COMPONENT OF THE ARMED FORCES, BRING EVIDENCE WITH YOU. IF YOU WEAR GLASSES, BRING THEM. IF MARRIED, BRING PROOF OF YOUR MARRIAGE. IF YOU HAVE ANY PHYSICAL OR MENTAL CONDITION WHICH, IN YOUR OPINION, MAY DISQUALIFY YOU FOR SERVICE IN THE ARMED FORCES, BRING A PHYSICIAN'S CERTIFICATE DESCRIBING THAT CONDITION, IF NOT ALREADY FURNISHED TO YOUR LOCAL BOARD.

Valid documents are required to substantiate dependency claims in order to receive basic allowance for quarters. Be sure to take the following with you when reporting to the induction station. The documents will be returned to you. (a) FOR LAWFUL WIFE OR LEGITIMATE CHILD UNDER 21 YEARS OF AGE—original, certified copy or photostat of a certified copy of marriage certificate, child's birth certificate, or a public or church record of marriage issued over the signature and seal of the custodian of the church or public records; (b) FOR LEGALLY ADOPTED CHILD—certified court order of adoption; (c) FOR CHILD OF DIVORCED SERVICE MEMBER (Child in custody of person other than claimant)—(1) Certified or photostatic copies of receipts from custodian of child evidencing serviceman's contributions for support, and (2) Divorce decree, court support order or separation order; (d) FOR DEPENDENT PARENT—affidavits establishing that dependency.

Bring your Social Security Account Number Card. If you do not have one, apply at nearest Social Security Administration Office. If you have life insurance, bring a record of the insurance company's address and your policy number. Bring enough clean clothes for 3 days. Bring enough money to last 1 month for personal purchases.

This Local Board will furnish transportation, and meals and lodging when necessary, from the place of reporting to the induction station where you will be examined. If found qualified, you will be inducted into the Armed Forces. If found not qualified, return transportation and meals and lodging when necessary, will be furnished to the place of reporting.

You may be found not qualified for induction. Keep this in mind in arranging your affairs, to prevent any undue hardship if you are not inducted. If employed, inform your employer of this possibility. Your employer can then be prepared to continue your employment if you are not inducted. To protect your right to return to your job if you are not inducted, you must report for work as soon as possible after the completion of your induction examination. You may jeopardize your reemployment rights if you do not report for work at the beginning of your next regularly scheduled working period after you have returned to your place of employment.

Willful failure to report at the place and hour of the day named in this Order subjects the violator to fine and imprisonment. Bring this Order with you when you report.

If you are so far from your own local board that reporting in compliance with this Order will be a serious hardship, go immediately to any local board and make written request for transfer of your delivery for induction, taking this Order with you.

SSS Form 252 (Revised 4-28-65)   (Previous printings may be used until exhausted.)

"Yea, a Letter from the President"
My induction Letter from Richard Nixon.

"Can I Go Home Now"
Mom, Dad and me at Fort Dix NJ. during boot camp. My
Dad was a combat medic in WW11 and was proud that I
was carrying on the tradition. I love and miss them.

"My Dad"
He was a golden gloves fighter and WW11
Medic and the family protector.

CHAPTER 4
TRIAGE A-GO-GO

Ten weeks earlier

My next stop was at Fort Sam Houston in San Antonio where medics were trained. I arrived with two of my Rhode Island buddies, Richard, a chiropractor, and Paul, a high school dropout who was a little unstable to say the least. My roommate, Lawrence, was an African American from Louisiana who seemed to have an inbred hatred for white people. I thought he was all fired up from the "black is beautiful" movement. We had a shaky relationship although he tolerated me better than most white guys with whom he interacted. Our first night together was marked by words and a shoving and punching match that was only halted by two drill sergeants after thirty minutes of battle. Our sentence was to remain roommates for the entire ten weeks of training. He was a powerfully built man with huge arms. Although we had several more encounters before we went our separate ways, we ended up respecting each other.

I was again selected to be a platoon leader and would march my unit to and from mess hall. I apparently didn't learn much from my short career as the platoon leader at Fort Dix. One day, I decided to be cool and let the troops sing some off-color songs while marching and letting them have a good time. A passing officer saw our antics and reported the platoon. I was immediately stripped of my grade and sent back into the ranks.

Despite my misgivings that as a medic I'd have a target mark on my back, I decided to throw myself wholeheartedly into the training since

I had a new seriousness of purpose. Lives would depend on how well I learned medical treatment just in case I was sent to Vietnam, a fate that I still was trying to avoid.

There's no doubt about it that being a medic is a noble calling. An army combat medic provides medical treatment to wounded troops on the battlefield as well as assisting in inpatient care at makeshift hospitals a.k.a. smelly green tents. Looking forward to learning the necessary medical skills, I wondered how I would react to stressful situations with bullets and mortars flying in the air. After all, the closest to tension that I ever had was standing on a free throw line with a basketball game tied.

The Advanced Individual Training was to last ten weeks. Classroom lectures taught us basic first aid to triage, a system used to identify casualties in terms of severity. Movies and slides ran pretty constantly, showing us one gory event after another. Sometimes I was distracted by my need to calm my stomach from a heave ho. For some reason, the most gruesome films were shown after lunch. Nothing could distract me, however, from the realization that the choices made in triage could lead to death sentences for some combat troops. I studied the medical books a lot, hoping that the pages would teach me anatomy and medicine through osmosis.

Nonetheless, I was hoping for some hands-on training for grievous wounds, but it never came. There was no internship in a hospital or troop clinic. Instead, the hands-on training had us sewing towels together as an exercise in suturing. Inoculating oranges was the training tool to teach us how to administer morphine or set up intravenous lines. As time went on, the medic training made me more and more insecure about my skills and readiness for field medicine. I felt it was ludicrous to puncture orange skins as a substitution for inoculations into real skin, but when I looked around at my colleagues, nobody seemed to have an issue with it. I felt woefully unprepared to work on battered bodies and how to evacuate fallen soldiers from the war zone. My insecurity fueled my desire that somehow I wouldn't be sent to 'Nam but to an office to file reports because of my business background from Bryant College. I actually prayed that somebody in authority would recognize that with my education, I would be better suited for office work. Maybe I'd be stationed at a hospital outside of Vietnam to receive soldiers transported there for care.

We trained in earnest for jungle warfare. Part of our training was also getting us used to carrying both our soldier equipment and medical supplies. Our first-aid packs had the usual stuff like sunblock, aspirin, bandages, etc., but also tourniquets, six vials of morphine, antibiotics, scissors, scalpels, and IV lines. Hauling a carbine, magazine clips, and a firearm had added heft to my rucksack and shoulders. I saw myself as a combatant as well as a medic. I wouldn't hesitate to return Charlie's fire when the time came, so I didn't scrimp on weaponry. We would go out into the rain for maneuvers that entailed crawling with medical supplies on our backs as well as fighting gear weighing in total sums of 65–70 lbs. while live ammo whistled over our heads.

I could only imagine the real thing happening in battle, and I knew I had to make sure that it wasn't going to be a reality for me. Every day, I would talk with various army personnel in various clerks' jobs and to my superiors to sell myself for getting a position in that field. I figured that I was in a good position to be a paper pusher in the US or some other country, just putting in my time until discharge.

All in all, Fort Houston was a really pretty place with the Alamo right down the road. We even got to see some great shows in the city like Janis Joplin and Neil Diamond although the residents seemed to hate the army since it was an air force town. Yet I felt in a time warp.

Training was tedious, and life in the barracks amounted to endless days of remembering the past and wondering what was ahead of us. Still, most of us never ever thought about whether we would end up as war detritus. I didn't call home much in those days because of my embarrassment of not graduating, but my thoughts were always centered on my family. Toward the end of medical training, the time seemed to drag on even more slowly, and we were all ready to get the hell out of Ft. Houston. We had our final exam of poking oranges and sewing towels together, and we all seemed to pass.

At the end of the training, Richard had finally persuaded the brass at Ft. Sam's to keep him on the base. The higher-ups had copped an attitude that a chiropractor wasn't a real doctor because his kind of medicine wasn't acknowledged by the American Medical Association. He managed to make himself indispensable and got rostered as a trainer for the duration of his tenure. I was destined to be a failure at my lobbying for a clerk's job and for my backup position to remain out of the war arena.

Shortly before we were to get our assignments, our beloved sergeant told us that we had a three-day leave that would start immediately. Our sprits rose as we considered the options we had in the city. My initial impression that the city folk were inhospitable to army became even more confirmed. My buddies and I started hitting drinking establishments only to find a cold reception wherever we went. At the Golden Peacock, a local watering hole, we almost met our waterloo when we tried to familiarize ourselves with the local women. We found ourselves surrounded by twenty or so air force personnel who laid claim to the harem of lovelies. Being outnumbered twenty to five, we put up a game account of ourselves, but in the end, we escaped out the back door with a few cut lips and shiners.

As we hurriedly left with our lives intact, we met up with a Mexican opportunist who would take us on a ride we would never forget.

Right over the border, he informed us, was a paradise for military personnel where we would be treated like kings for the right price. We needed an ego boost, so away we went for fun and adventure. As we passed the border into Nuevo Laredo, we were almost knocked out by the odor that hung in the air. There was no way I was going to eat or drink anything here except for Corona Beer in the bottle where the cap was taken off in front of me.

Anyway, we went on an old oxen buckboard pulled by two donkeys into the Laredo desert, which had to be at least 100 degrees heat and where only sagebrush and scorpions could have a happy life. All of a sudden, an old fort stood like a mirage ahead in the middle of nowhere, and we wondered what was inside the gates. The large front doors were dragged open, and there stood a mystical city with one side looking like a seedy Las Vegas and the other side of the road looking like a picture from an old Western movie.

We were left off on the Las Vegas side of town and entered one of the clubs. Wall-to-wall GIs and wall-to-wall gorgeous women were scattered all over the establishment. It seemed surreal in a country were poverty abounded. Upon sitting at a table, we were joined by several beautiful senoritas who became real friendly in a hurry. They tried everything to entice us to surrender some hard cash for their services. There was no way to tell how old they were, but they were sent out to this boys town when they were very young to bring home some money for the survival of their families. This side of the road was government inspected, as we were told by the United States, for diseases, and they were all registered with the locals. The cost for a fling was $6–$8, and we all ended up taking advantage of the situation in one way or another. Thus began my rationalization, which I would carry into Vietnam, that I was helping the women to step out of poverty.

After hitting several of the clubs in this high-rent district, my buddies and I crossed the street to a world that is hard to describe. Along the beaten-down road were little grass shacks with just enough protection to keep out the afternoon sun from frying eggs on you head. Outside these dwellings were women of every age and shape offering all kinds of goodies for $1–$2. Anything that went on this side of the proverbial tracks with no government oversight was at our own risk. In one shack, one woman was servicing men while her children were playing in the next room, and the shack next door had several women putting on erotic shows for a GI. Most bizarre was that of a woman doing everything possible with a donkey while strapped to the animal's belly. It was a coin toss as to what was sickest, the woman or the GIs encouraging such a display by paying her. There were lots of other things going on in the shacks, and we spent the better part of the day like voyeurs ourselves, exploring the sights and sounds of boys town. Out of money after a few hours in Mexico, we started back with a sense of amazement at what we had experienced but also sadness of what people in other countries must do to survive. I also privately kept my personal shame to myself at having been a participant.

The big day arrived at last when we would finally find out where we would spend the next twelve months of our duty. We were all called to the parade grounds to hear the news of where we would be traveling from here and the thousand or so of us inductees were waiting, thinking of family back home and whether or not we were going to see them again. Some guys around me had an Audie Murphy complex and bragged about going home at the end of their tours to a big ticker tape parade in their small town with medals brandished on their chests to those of us who just wanted to get the whole thing over with. I wanted to get back to my parents and Kathy, my girlfriend, and finish my degree and make them all proud of me. There were several destinations *possible* for medics besides 'Nam, like Korea or in the stateside army hospitals. I had little hope by now since the previous class all headed to Southeast Asia. As names were called alphabetically, a few guys got other posts, but by the time they got to S, there was a steady stream of assignments to Vietnam.

"Pfc. James Squadrito, Vietnam."

It shocked me a little, but what could I do? And besides, I really didn't know what I was really getting into but I would soon find out.

I hadn't realized that we were going to have some liberty, but we were all sent home for two weeks before reporting to Oakland, California, for our twenty-three-hour flight to the "Unpromised Land." I had mixed feelings about returning to Rhode Island because I knew my dad was still hurting from the news of my college demise. I was overjoyed when I was met at the airport back home when my father embraced me warmly. I knew then that he wanted me to know that he was behind me, and I assured him that I would finish my degree upon my return.

It was a great homecoming for the two weeks with my family and friends hosting parties for me, but my mom was very sad and was having trouble handling the situation. She had watched the TV news religiously and was well versed on the casualties of the war. Each fatality she learned about became a harbinger of things to come for her son. She was under medication by the family doctor, and I feared that she could not take much more pain in her life. I told her a little white lie that I was going to spend my tour in an army MASH (mobile army surgical hospital) unit in Saigon, but somehow, I knew that she didn't believe a word of it.

My reunion with my girlfriend Kathy went well. She promised to wait for me and would send me a letter each day. She was a first-year teacher and loved her job. She said it distracted her from thinking about the worst for me. Needless to say, I omitted any reference to my trip to Mexico.

The two weeks flew by, and I said my good-byes. Away I jetted to the Oakland Army Dispatch Center for processing. The barracks were jammed full of army grunts waiting for transfer, and every day, several hundred would leave on that infamous Peter, Paul, and Mary's jet plane.

The night before my flight, I joined a few guys for a sweep of the tenderloin section of San Francisco, and it turned out to be an adventure. We hit several clubs along the strip and saw some unusual acts and met some weird people. At one establishment, some beautiful ladies asked us to buy them a glass of wine. They were so nice to be with after spending days with grubby GIs, so we were fast to order the drinks. After they finished their bubbly, they danced off to another table and gave some other guys the same lines. We decided to leave and ask for the bill. When it came, we couldn't believe our eyes, $750 for three glasses of wine. We had no intention of paying that amount, so I asked for the manager. He told us to pay up or else. We ended up knocking down the bouncers and fleeing the joint, leaving $100 for the bill before the cops arrived. Hell, we were going to 'Nam. Who cared if we were put in jail anyway?

I left the main group and decided to go solo at a great-looking night-club on one of the side streets in Frisco. I sat at the bar and marveled at all of the hot babes hanging around. All of a sudden, the most beautiful lady I ever saw came up to me and said hi. Her name was Roberta, and she had everything you could ever want in a woman, and it certainly was an ego boost getting attention from that lady. We sat and talked and danced away the few hours, and of course, I parted with some big bucks for the pleasure of her company. She asked me to come over to her apartment to spend the evening. I was flattered that such a beauty would even consider being with a shaved-head geek like me.

We left the club and started walking to her place when, all of a sudden, a sergeant from across the street ran over and pushed Roberta on the ground and hit her across the face. I was outraged and started to scuffle with him until he did something I wasn't ready for. He grabbed Roberta's hair and ripped it off my lovely lady's head only to unveil a good-looking guy in drag. My stomach was turning as I remembered all the dancing and kissing we did for hours and the prospect of what would have happened when I finally noticed what was under her dress.

These transvestites were called Murphys in that section of town, and I can tell you that nobody could tell the difference between them and a female movie star. The only reason why the sergeant knew was because he had been with her/him the evening before, and when he got to her apartment, her partner in crime mugged him. We called the police and had a big laugh over the incident, and I was happy that I never got to be with Roberta/Robert, and never felt beneath that dress. The sergeant's name was Tim, and I found out he was from Central Falls, Rhode Island. We hit as few more clubs that night and ended up with two ladies who were twenty years older than us and spent a night enjoying their company. The next morning, we headed back to Oakland to begin our introduction to the horror of war.

CHAPTER 5

FIRST STOP

It looked like the inverse of the Fourth of July celebration back in my hometown as reds fired rockets exploded below amid puffs of smoke except this was midday in December 1969 and my plane was descending into a hell hole called Bien Hoa, Vietnam. I thought it quite ironic that one of the biggest song hits in 1969 was Peter, Paul, and Mary's "Leaving on a Jet Plane." A voice from the cockpit told us grunts that we'd be on the ground in ten minutes.

"Exit quickly," he barked, "and locate a ditch around the perimeter. Wait until the all-clear signal to rear your ugly heads."

The transport skidded down the runway, bouncing a couple a ties amid rockets buzzing. As a basketball cocaptain and guard, I never moved as fast and I dove into the closest hole. Jammed in with a dozen guys, I was shaking. Two other recruits next to me looked like they had St. Vitus dance, and I hoped that I wasn't as transparently scared as they were. Several GI Joe gung-ho types to my right were screaming how they wanted to kill a gook on their first day.

A rocket landed two feet away, rattling my bones and shutting them up. Rockets continued to whoosh by. Some helicopters from the base loomed overhead and bombarded the wooded area around us. It was quite a drubbing.

There was a moment of silence. A siren sounded. Was this the all-clear signal? Nobody moved.

"Get your fuckin' asses outta the ditch," a voice blared over a loud-speaker. We scrambled up, and a sergeant pointed to a huge tent area where we'd be processed for further duty. Lines were long except in my queue. I was the only one. After checking my papers, the sergeant whistled for a jeep and told me to get on it. I was headed for Lai Khe, the support aid station for the troops in surrounding areas.

I was struck that the road was pretty good for traveling. We passed acres and acres of rice paddies with Vietnamese peasants working the fields. We passed through several villages where the people eyed us with inscrutable looks. I saw a few signs that were handwritten with the word Massage on them. I didn't think that it meant you could get a massage there only that it was a similar word, meaning something or other. I'd soon find out what it meant.

What was weird about the visuals was the contrasting conflict to one's senses. I really couldn't talk to the driver. I couldn't even hear myself speak because of the explosions and artillery fire off in the distance. The extreme heat made me perspire so much that my fatigues were soaked within minutes. Perspiration soaked through to my skin, and I couldn't stop the steady stream of water dripping from my forehead. The stench in the air almost choked me. There were no sewer systems in 'Nam, and human feces were put in piles and doused with gasoline. The Vietnamese would then set the dung on fire so the entire sky was a dark cloud that stank of crap. I wanted to catch the next plane out, but I knew that the only exit was for me to finish my tour or leave on a stretcher or body bag.

As we got closer to the base, I could hear the *tick, tick, tick* of gunfire coming from the right side of the road. I jumped a bit. My driver, Roger, shouted, "No sweat. Just duck." When we entered the sentry gates at Lai Khe, I got out of the vehicle after clearance. I noticed a number of bullet hits just below my window. I asked Roger if these were new, and he nodded yes and laughed. I thought to myself that I almost didn't make it through the first day. Thinking of home and the girl I left behind, I wanted to get this over as quickly as possible. I knew I was kidding myself, of course, since I was in for a long haul. We arrived at the support station and my medical evacuation unit.

My first job was to meet the helicopters carrying the wounded and to transport them to this unit. The tags for priorities of treatment were already on the stretchers since the initial decision regarding care was made by the evacuating medics. A radio op would announce when the choppers were five minutes away, and we would race out to the fields to meet them. The movie version of *MASH* I had just seen featuring Donald Sutherland, Elliot Gould, and Sally Kellerman right there on the base with the projector sending the pictures to a sheet stretched between two trees, so the drill here was pretty similar. This aspect of the job I did fairly well until I saw Specialist Marshall and this experience.

The day before Specialist Marshall's arrival, I had unloaded a stretcher with three bodies in piles all burned to unrecognizable states. I cried so loudly that I embarrassed myself. It only got worse. Forty or fifty other bodies were carried into the morgue located in a bunker near the station. I, along with other medics, had to identify the soldiers, but most of the time, it was impossible. We found dog tags but didn't know who the owners were. As I looked on these young kids lying in pools of blood and guts, my mind wandered into the dimension of picturing myself on one of the stretchers since I would shortly go out on patrol. I had no sleep that night with visions of mutilated bodies in my head. Thereafter, the most I slept was two hours a night during my entire tour.

During my tenure at the aid station, I unloaded hundreds of bodies both dead and alive. The frustration was enormous when we could not identify them. There was a grave registrar with whom we worked with, trying to put a name with the corpse, many times, unsuccessfully.

What happened though on that first day of unloading bodies might have gotten me court-martialed early in my career. The horrible siren had rung again, and we unloaded the charred remains. The smell of death hovered over us as only a few survivors were pulled off the 'copters. All of a sudden, a major came barreling into the aid station and demanded,

"How many gooks did we kill?" He had to do a kill report to his commander. At no time amid the bodies of our own soldiers did he ask about how his men were or even talk a small amount to the survivors from the firefight. I felt like rearranging his face but muttered a profanity at him instead. I'm sure he heard my epithet but chose to ignore my comment. For weeks, I could see the faces of my comrades, who had given their lives in battle, lying there while this joker looked good at the Pentagon with his kill report.

One time when I was doing identities, I became disturbed by something I found out. On one cart were two bodies of black soldiers with bullet holes through the back of their respective necks. Initially, it intrigued me that the Vietcong could get that close to inflict the damage. I retrieved their dog tags and several bracelets from them and other deceased soldiers so that loved ones at home could have a memento or two along with someone to bury. While my job was merely to put the items and ID into plastic bags, I was still uneasy about the wounds on the two men of color.

One of my fellow medics was a guy named Billy Roach. He had been in the country for eleven months and knew everything about what was going in the area. I told him my concern and asked him to take a look. He agreed that the wounds were inflicted at short range, which meant the enemy had to be right on top of the soldiers. Upon examination, the wound was made by an American weapon not a Vietcong gun. According to Billy, who had seen this many times before, the deaths were a result of an execution, not a Vietcong hit. This was one more example of the white versus black war that was continuing unabated and growing.

The remaining times during my tour of duty, I was busy doing autopsies. This was the easiest task for me. When I was seventeen, I worked to make money for school. The then hourly wage, I think, was $1.09 per hour. The memorial hospital which was located two and one-half miles from my home was offering $5.00 per hour for an autopsy assistant. My job was to receive the organs from the medical examiner and put them on scales for weighing. I was on call 24/7, and many a night, I was called to the hospital. In one year, I had assisted in forty-two autopsies.

The experience was not, however, without its scars. I had to walk to the hospital, and many a night, my overactive imagination scared the bejesus out of me. The rustling trees and bushes en route made me think that demons lurked. I sometimes had nightmares.

I mentioned my roommate earlier. He was a first-class character. He was nicknamed Reverend Randy Rooney. I saw his effects before I saw him. The hooch was loaded with religious artifacts and shrines upon my arrival. He had candles all over the place.

He entered with a Bible in his hand and gave me a cold stare. He popped on some religious music, which sounded like chant, and he played it so loudly, it was splitting my eardrums. I asked him to pipe it down. He asked if I needed anything, and when I said no, he told me that he would discuss my spiritual situation when he returned. He abruptly left. I put down my rucksack on the floor and noticed my brown blanket moving. I jokingly wondered if he had spiritual kinesis. As I approached my bunk for a closer look the blanket became alive and hundreds of roaches the size of small birds flew at me and covered me in a hurry. I ran outside to the laughter of a gathering of longtimers who wanted to get their jollies from watching a "fuckin' new guy," a.k.a. FNG, in terror. From that day forward, I would always keep my mosquito netting fastened firmly around my bed.

As pesky as the roaches were, Rev. Randy was more of a pest. He was a self-ordained minister who would work on me for hours to convert me to the Lord. He kept telling me that I was going to hell unless I repented for my sins. Every night, he would read the Bible for hours and light candles to seek God's forgiveness. I couldn't help but respect him for his beliefs, and he was really sort of amusing, but my mind was on how to survive the next eleven months in the country.

One night, another medic and I sneaked ten ladies from the local village into one of the bunkers and began to blow off steam. One of the corporals, Dave Tuttle, looking for advancement, took it upon himself to inform the military police of our actions. The MPs came storming in, and my buddy and I received Article 15s and an extra day's duty. In retaliation, we planned a special party for Dave. Several days after the incident, we went into the jungle and gathered every insect known to man. There were spiders as big as your hands, twelve-inch centipedes, flying roaches, biting red ants, along with every slimy and slithering thing we could find. We collected thousands of these creatures and put them in a large barrel. While he slept one evening, we quietly entered his abode and let loose the whole army of these critters on him in the bunk. I never heard screams like that in my life, but he never finked on us again except for one more time when his memory and sanity momentarily left him.

The reverend, however, chastised me good and proper for my uncharitable act.

Reverend Randy was a hell of a medic, no matter what you thought about his religious bent. He actually did give me succor one evening. We were on night duty at the station when we heard the sound we hated most, helicopter blades signaling more wounded or dead soldiers were coming. Reverend Randy, his Bible in one hand, and I raced to the 'copters. He and I picked up a stretcher carrying the parts of four GIs. I saw tears streaming down his face as he read scripture, and my heart was pounding as we reached for another stretcher. This one had two bodies, one an African American man that had his head severed from his body and another body with only the torso. I lost it, and threw up behind a row of trees. At that point, I was only in the horrors of war under a month, and it was getting to me. Reverend Randy came up to me and read a calming psalm from the Bible. As much as I used to consider him a pain in the ass, he seemed to know what to read to calm my inner soul. When more casualties arrived the next night, Rev's soothing scripture for some reason kept me sane that night and most of the time thereafter.

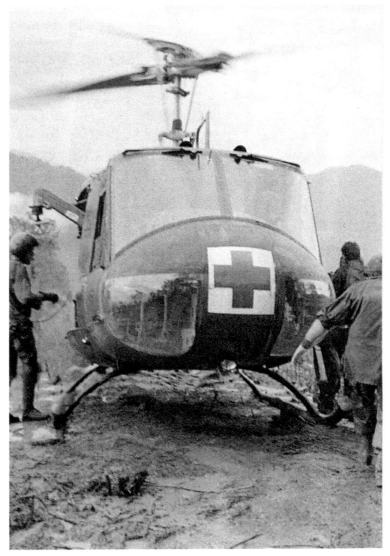

"Visions of My New Job"
Day and night choppers kept coming, bringing
the wounded and the dead.

"The Wounded's Best Friend"
Chopper Pilots were always there to bring our
heroes back for medical assistance.

"Safety in Numbers"
Helicopters helping to clear the area after
attacks were always a welcomed site.

CHAPTER 6
TRUST NOBODY

When I arrived at this first assignment, it wasn't long before I was schooled by my fellow GIs as to the facts of life in Vietnam. Shortly before my arrival, there had been a fierce fight known as the Tet Offensive with most of the attack centered on Saigon and Da Nang. Soldiers who had been there for the battle spoke of their many comrades who were killed or maimed during the long siege. There were still many soldiers in hospital beds injured and without limbs as a result of that sneak attack.

The Tet Offensive was fodder for the hatred on the part of our troops for the North Vietnamese soldiers and the Vietcong. Tet, the Vietnamese New Year, occurs somewhere in the last few days of January into February for twenty days. In the Vietnamese culture, it is a combination of Thanksgiving, Christmas, New Year's and Easter as it would be comparably in the West.

The overall customs of the Tet celebration for the people begin by cleaning and decorating the homes – Children are given the task to make the home clean and to put elaborate decorations on the walls and outside the home.

They then adorn themselves with new clothes – The whole family gets new clothes for the celebration with the best outfit being worn on the first day of the celebration.

Bid farewell to the kitchen god (Ong Tao) – Vietnamese families pray for the kitchen god to go up to heaven and report to the Jade Emperor about the affairs of that family for the year.

Giao Thua (New Year's Eve) – During the passage of the old year to the new year, the first houseguest to offer a greeting is the most important. If the guest has a good aura then the family will have good luck and fortune for the year. Otherwise, a bad aura guarantees just the opposite.

Apricot and peach flowers – These symbolize new beginnings. The apricot (*hoa mai*) is good in warm weather and the peach (*hoa dao*) is good for cold weather. These flowers are on display during the Tet.

Giving away red envelopes – These symbolize wealth and luck. The family elders give envelopes with money to the young.

Offering to ancestors – On the first day before the celebration, noontime offerings of food, wine, cakes, fruit, and burning incense are set aside for the ancestors.

Finally, the Tet tree – Preparation comes to an end with the raising of the New Year's tree.

As the saying goes, on paper, the idea looked good. The Americans apparently got suckered in by thinking that this most important period for the Vietnamese, which is rooted on peace, would be a quiet time on the front. There also was a cease fire period declared for the holiday celebration, which had been initiated by the North Vietnamese and agreed to by the South Vietnamese command, which in 1968 began on January 30. The enemy also calculated that this would be what the Americans were concluding, so they planned a fierce attack while soldiers had their guard down. Loaded with every available weapon, usually supplied by China, the Vietnamese army charged the outposts and bases then the Vietcong attacked the cities in South Vietnam in a well-planned, orchestrated movement.

The first surprise attack was at Khe Sanh, which turned out to be a diversionary tactic to take American attention away from the major cities. Forces were moved out of the city to the neighboring environs. The battle tactic was largely successful as a military and political operation. The North Vietnamese Army wanted to give a sense of victory to its people to shore up the populace's fading support for the war. Additionally, it wanted to dishearten the South Vietnamese living in the major cities that were largely insulated from the rigors of war.

The National Liberation Front (the Vietcong, also called Charlie) then attacked the cities and the provinces throughout South Vietnam. Many American as well as South Vietnamese troops were on respective leaves and cancelling them came too late. During the fight, communist forces mortared or rocketed every major allied airfield and attacked dozens of district capitals in the south. Some urban areas were temporarily seized by enemy. Some Vietcong made it to the American Embassy but did not get inside the building.

The United States and the South Vietnamese troops would eventually stop the advance but huge casualties abounded. In attacking Saigon, where many journalists took up residence, the Vietcong opened up the power of the press. Stories of war dominated the headlines back in the states. Protests by American students and other surged during the attack. Both sides suffered casualties, but the Communists saw the worst of it, that is, except for the civilians in these areas. Bodies of the innocent South Vietnamese people were front and center in magazines and newspapers, thereby fanning protests in the United States.

Bitterly, the soldiers talked about the fact that a gook could never be trusted as a result of this supposed cease-fire. "Cram the peace thing," they warned us newbies.

"Not a one of them can be trusted. Assume villagers would like to see our throats slit."

The Tet was supposed to be a celebration of family and ancestors in heaven. For our troops, however, and for the South Vietnamese army and civilians, it was an unforgettable lesson and a visit to hell.

For me, listening to the quite literally war stories, I became slightly paranoid and vowed never to let my defenses down. I would not, however, always keep that resolution.

CHAPTER 7
LIFE INSIDE THE CAMP

Days were long and hot at the frontline aid station in La Khe. Running to and from choppers with the wounded and the dead was mentally fatiguing. Attending to the wounded made me feel like I was doing something good in my life, but I was afraid and lonely like most soldiers in my group.

The one alleviation from the usual work was a once-a-week movie from the good old US of A. We never knew what movie we'd be getting, but as long as there were round-eyed movie stars in it, we were happy. The first one I saw in 1969 was a film starring Catherine Deneuve and Jack Lemmon called *April Fools*. We strung some wire between two trees in the compound and attached a sheet. Jack Lemmon was super, but Ms. Deneuve was out-of-this-world gorgeous. After the movie, most of us were starstruck and wrote her letters. If she ever got our fan mail, she never wrote back which, of course, made us the April fools. Oh well, at least we could dream of being with her.

One of the weirdest pictures I saw was *The Illustrated Man* with Rod Steiger. It was the story of a man who had a tattoo on his back that when you looked at it, you would see how and when you were going to die. None of us wanted to look at anything like that because we never knew when our time was to pass, and we didn't want to know. I wondered what sadist had chosen that movie delight for us.

We loved though these touches from home, which included some film debuts that hadn't been seen stateside yet. I would get sad, however, when the picture ended.

One other thing made me curious about the movie selection. Films like *The Great White Hope* with James Earl Jones were shown. That made me a bit nervous because of the black-white tensions always simmering on the base.

Besides the movies, there wasn't much recreation other than the exercises to keep one alive at our base. I lucked out one day when I helped an army engineer beat a particularly virulent case of VD (venereal disease) with some potent medication. Since he was married, he didn't want his affliction on a medical record, so I didn't record it. When his disease cleared up, he told me that he would do something nice for all of us in the future.

Shortly thereafter, several large engineer trucks pulled up at our location. The men climbed out and put together a basketball court for us. Everybody was going crazy, including me, because it brought back memories of home. A large box was delivered to my hooch with a large letter that said, "Thanks! Here's the something nice I promised you." Inside were six basketballs! I was happy that I had told him I was a basketball fanatic dating back to my college days!

We played on that court as much as possible between patrols and guarding the perimeter. There was nary a time when GIs weren't dunking baskets. We heard that a hospital unit in the rear had a team, so we challenged them to a game. We invited everybody to watch the contest, so sure were we that we'd massacre them since they had to be eggheads. We didn't know that the hospital's players were ex-college standouts that were picked to stay in the rear for the amusement of the top brass. They slaughtered us by forty-five points. Never did the adage that pride cometh before a fall have more meaning for me.

The biggest recreation on the base was taking dope. Whether it was heroin or marijuana, all 100 percent pure if it was the real thing, the drugs freely flowed with the brass ignoring the problem. Virtually every day, we would hear the sirens signifying a rocket attack. Newbies like me would hunker in our bunkers, praying that our time wasn't up. You could easily spot the guys who were in the country the longest because they would be on top of the bunkers, smoking a J and admiring the beautiful red glare of the exploding rockets. The attacks were only a few minutes, but to me, they seemed to be an eternity. When I'd emerge subsequently after the attack, I would see the old-timers laughing and whooping it up without having taken any cover.

Taking drugs in Vietnam was like eating popcorn at the movies. It was easily attainable, and the price was usually right. Vietnamese boys, ages six to ten would carry backpacks full of pure weed and sell it. Often, the Vietcong would put the children up to selling the Americans the drugs, which were usually toxic. It was a smart plan of attack. Many of these kids were orphans because their parents were either in the war as Vietcong or dead. GIs would buy the heroin or marijuana from the children lined up just outside the wire perimeter.

Reverend and I would try to keep the kids safe, but many of them were killed for not delivering money to the Vietcong that they had gotten from soldiers who needed a fix. I personally assisted at autopsies where soldiers died because the heroin was laced with battery acid. The reports back home would tell the loved ones that they had died in action, but the truth was that many of them died of tainted drugs.

Reverend Randy and I felt sorry for these kids forced into the trade game by the enemy to attack our weaknesses from within. Many a battle within a soldier's own body was as fierce as that with the Vietcong on the battlefield. One day, Randy and I saw a kid about two hundred yards from our fence being beaten by adults. I, and several others, grabbed weapons and headed over to help the youngster. His head was profusely bleeding, and he couldn't walk too well. We chased away his tormenters and brought him into the aid station. He had a concussion and a leg fracture. Through a South Vietnamese interpreter, we found out that he was only six years old and had been dealing drugs for the Vietcong for over a year. He was trembling and scared because he thought that we would treat him worse than his own people would. In his eyes, he had been brainwashed to believe that we were the devil incarnate.

The South Vietnamese wanted to take him into custody, but we decided to keep him under medical watch for a while. We got attached to this little guy, whom we called Yoyo, and he seemed to understand that we were looking out for his wellbeing. Through the interpreter, he told us how badly the children were being treated and how young girls as young as eleven or twelve were put out as prostitutes. This made me sick, but I also realized that US soldiers were also rationalizing about their sexual activities with young girls. Far too many times, I heard GIs excusing sex with preteens on the basis that these girls would probably be married off by age fourteen anyway.

About a month after Yoyo came to us, a South Vietnamese soldier took custody of him since he seemed to know a lot about the location of the Vietcong soldiers. We never saw him again.

Nonetheless, drug use continued uninterrupted on the base. The brass seemed to condone its use since it was so blatantly used.

There was one guy in the unit, Tom Myerson, who was about 6'4" and weighed about 260 lbs. We called him Buddha because people came to him for information and comfort, mostly in the form of drugs. During my time, he had the most experience in the country and knew all the ins and outs of how to survive. He was *the* supplier of girls and weed through connections he had with local villages. Buddha would take an army vehicle through the gates and trade supplies usually given to him by the unit's chef, the Soupman. He would then sell the bounty to the camp and share the proceeds with the Soupman and officers who looked the other way.

Being part of Buddha's inner circle was the aspiration of most medics in camp. I got there by parlaying the bundles of joy my mother would send, which were full of delights from home. I had received a letter from her telling me that the biggest bundle was on its way. The days dragged by as I waited her home-cooked meals.

Finally, the box arrived, and I was called to pick it up. After it was checked out, I rushed back to my hooch to see what Mama had sent me. There were loads of canned goods, particularly peaches, since I was crazy about them; franks and beans; bread pudding; canned ham; homemade cookies; and lots more. But the pièce de résistance was on the bottom of the box wrapped in a package. With Reverend looking over my shoulder, I unwrapped it, hoping to find something that would bring some sanity to my existence here.

As I peeled back the wrapping, I could see the images of four young men marching in a row. No! It can't be. Yes yes, it is! Good gracious God! It was the Beatles' album, *Abbey Road*. That was gold! That was the ticket to the Super Bowl.

Those four Brits had taken America by storm in 1969. All of us had heard about them from letters from home and magazines sent to the troops. *Abbey Road* was the holy grail since it was difficult to secure that chronically sold out album.

I raced over to Buddha's hooch to show him. He slapped me on the back! It would be the perfect songs to smoke pot and get lost in the music.

During the daily visits to his hooch, the album played over and over again with the J hanging heavily in the air. I heard the album so many times that I remembered the songs in order: "Come Together," "Something," "Maxwell's Silver Hammer," "Oh! Darling," "Octopus's Garden," "I Want You," "Here Comes the Sun," "Because," "You Never Give Me Your Money," "Sun King," "Mean Mr. Mustard," "Polythene Pam," "She Came in through the Bathroom Window," "Golden Slumbers," "Carry That Weight," "The End," and "Her Majesty."

That was truly music to get high on.

I did not smoke marijuana although once, by mistake, I had marijuana. I was going out on patrol with a unit. The chef, the Soupman, gave me cookies to treat the troops. When we rested after a long patrol, I passed them out and ate the cookies also. I noticed some of my comrades acting funny. One guy was talking to a tree. In a bit, I felt dizzy. My wooziness didn't clear up until I was back at camp. The Soupman asked how I liked the treat. Not wanting to insult him, I said the cookies were fine. He whooped! He announced that he had got me stoned by cooking marijuana into the dessert!

In the hooch, the air was so dense with marijuana smoke that I couldn't help ingest some. But as a medic, I had seen accidents and men somewhat too impaired to perform, and I did not want any death or harm coming to somebody wounded because I didn't have a clear head. My morals only went so far, though. I was so lonely for home that I was desperate to have a "gang" to belong to. I went to Buddha's pad every chance I got for the camaraderie.

The Beatles album joined our stash of music at Buddha's. We had albums and singles from the Rolling Stones' "You Can't Always Get What You Want"; Elvis's "In the Ghetto"; the Hollies' "He Ain't Heavy, He's My Brother," which became sort of a theme song for us; the 5th Dimension's *Age of Aquarius*; Kenny Rogers's *Ruby, Don't Take Your Love to Town*, also an actual song about a paraplegic vet whose wife cheats on him; and of course, anything from Jimi Hendrix and Janis Joplin that we could get our hands on. In fact, when Hendrix and Joplin died, there was general mourning at our camp since, through their music, they had become our family.

One of the guys, Johnny Boy, had fingered a record player which I was surprised didn't wear out. The records were played at the highest volume as guys inhaled.

I should mention that Reverend didn't like my mother's gift at all. He knew that we would be doing things while the music was playing, which in his view would make God turn his head around from us. I half wondered that my mother would never have sent it if she knew this fact also. My mother and Reverend would have been allies! Many a time, Buddha procured mama-sans from the village to entertain us while the music blasted. From that service, I did not abstain.

Buddha had more Article 15s lodged at him than just about any-body. He seemed not to care. While he would lose some army checks, he'd make up the lost revenue through his side businesses.

One day while a group of soldiers, who were passing the pipe, and I were at Buddha's hooch, the first sergeant came in with an assignment. Because of Buddha's friendships with local villagers, he was asked to bring medical supplies to one town in exchange for information about the Vietcong. I was asked to accompany him on the trip. We took an army vehicle loaded with supplies and headed out the gate to a village some six miles from camp. As we got closer to our destination, I noticed that the sky was filled with smoke. I wanted to head back immediately, but Buddha wanted to pick up some weed for the guys and told me it was just the townspeople burning feces.

As we entered the village, we saw bodies lying all over, some wounded, some dead. The Vietcong had attacked the village and left these people in ruin because of their supposed friendship with the US. I knew that friendship was merely based on survival, which did not approximate any definition of friendship, but the Vietcong nonetheless retaliated. Also, we had received helpful information in the past from them, and I felt a duty to them.

We radioed back to the rear for support and started to give aid. Thankfully, we had a lot of supplies since we were toting them. Buddha and I did what we could to tie off arteries, using tourniquets, and clean-ing wounds. The work seemed endless.

Buddha was working on two small children when a large damaged tree started to give way and fell. He could not get totally clear, and the heaviest part of the trunk fell on his left leg. He lay there grimacing in pain. To mask his horrific pain, I gave him a shot of morphine, for which I knew that I'd have to answer for in the rear to the brass. I made a make-shift splint using a tree branch with bandages from my supply since I had used up all the splints I carried on some villagers. The backup team and security forces arrived, and we quickly cleaned up the carnage. Buddha's leg was broken in three places when we got him over to the MASH unit for X-rays.

The broken leg turned out to be a blessing in disguise for Buddha. Later that week, we would receive orders, and all of us, except him, would be sent to the frontlines. Buddha would spend the rest of his time in the rear hospital for a few months before being sent home.

I mentioned sex with villagers. This was something that the brass not only countenanced but actually encouraged. The network was extensive.

CHAPTER 8
CHARLIE'S ANGELS

I first noticed the massage parlors en route to the air support station. Those huts were actually brothels where GIs out in the field would queue up for sex. They were nicknamed, the Palace of Steam and Cream. The usual cost was $2. For those of us on the base, the girls were brought to us. Buddha and some other veteran medics would load up a vehicle with items like Salem cigarettes and candy and give the goods to the elders in the village. In turn, the elders would allow the women to accompany the medics back to the base.

The first time I saw this parade of women coming onto the base was one hot day shortly after my arrival. I was busy administering some penicillin to some GIs who had gone on their own into the village for sex and who had contracted some nasty STDs. The strain of VD in Vietnam was many times stronger than any caught stateside, and very high doses of medication were required to clear it up. Sometimes, treatment continued for several months. I asked another medic about the five women walking toward a couple of hooches. He told me he hadn't tested them, but apparently, another medic had, so they were clean. He went on the say that the brass approved a program of regular testing of the women who were servicing the GIs to make sure they were disease free. Later, I would do the screenings when I was assigned to Long Binh. I did lecture the soldiers, however, to use whiskey immediately after sex to wash the genital area and rush to the bathroom to force out a couple of drops of urine. Its acid would kill any incipient disease. My formula, which I learned from a master sergeant, was probably responsible for cutting half of the cases of venereal disease.

"Buddha's brought them in. They gotta be okay," the medic said with assurance. Buddha had not at this point injured his leg.

Two hooches were designated for the girls to work in, and a long line of soldiers stood waiting for his turn for $3, which was a buck more than in town since they were guaranteed clean. Buddha, who thought he knew everything there was to know about women, screwed up this time. The normal quick turnaround of services provided by the girls was slowed down because two of the girls were missing from the hooch and roaming the camp somewhere. This obviously was an obvious no-no, so Buddha began to panic when he could not locate them.

Charlie was aware of what was happening in our camp and all the camps in the country, so the enemy began to plant girls sympathetic to the North's cause in the villages where GIs would visit and trade. For the first time, I was about to experience the infiltration.

Buddha immediately informed the MPs, who supposedly were in the dark about these activities although they had let them through the gate, and even officers came out to search for the errant ladies. Several MPs who were searching behind the officer's quarters saw the girls taking something out of their large handbags that Buddha forgot to check. The women were quickly digging a hole in which to place this package. Before they could finish burying the pieces, the MPs swarmed in and detained the girls, stopping them in their tracks.

A bomb detonator specialist with the MPs carefully looked at each package and discovered that it was a satchel charge (explosives in a satchel with a detonator). Its size was big enough that it could have injured, maimed, or killed many officers had the girls completed their tasks. The girls were taken away, and the camp closed to all visitors. That did not last long since the needs of the soldiers trumped security. Yet the rhetoric flowed about never trusting any females in the village because they may end up as Charlie's angels.

Buddha and his buddies were taken for interrogation but subsequently cleared of the heavy charges by an army court although they got an Article 15 and a loss of pay. Ironically, the MPs and the senior officers when questioned as to whether they knew what Buddha was up to, and all denied knowledge. They got off scot-free. Buddha learned a lesson, or so he thought, on being extremely careful when dealing with the townspeople.

Within a week, the security fell lax again when other women returned to the base. I was asleep when I heard a loud bang coming from the back of the latrine. The whole camp was awakened and ran to see what happened.

It so happened that in the morning, one of the beloved mama-sans, Toa, from a tribe with whom we were friendly (by respecting their customs) with was helping us get a measure of cleanliness around camp by her doing the cleaning. The mama-sans worked in camps, doing jobs that the soldiers did not want to do, such as cleaning buildings, shining boots, doing laundry, filling sandbags at some bases, burning human waste, as well as giving some sexual services. Toa came from a nearby village and had ten children. We would give her food and money to help her take care of her family, and she returned the favor with love. She was not a prostitute.

As we approached the area where the blast seemed to emanate, we only hoped that she wasn't in the zone. One of the other mamas-sans who was a new arrival at camp was, however, a Vietcong sympathizer. She had buried explosives in an attempt to blow up the latrines while unsuspecting officers used the facilities. Toa saw her and tried to stop her. The explosives discharged killed the sympathizer and severely injuring Toa. Toa lost several fingers and a foot. After her recovery, she continued to provide the camp with TLC.

Heroes do come in many shapes and sizes and don't have to wear a uniform.

What made the monitoring of women coming and going to the camp difficult was the fact that Vietnamese women on our side came to the place to help us out. We Americans were not particularly adept at distinguishing women from the North or from the South since, to us, they all looked alike as far as their broad features went.

One day, the South Vietnamese army sent us a nurse to help out at the aid station and also to be an interpreter for South 'Nam soldiers whom we also treated. She was extremely beautiful. With the French occupation of Vietnam in the past, it changed not only the culture but made for a wonderful mix of Vietnamese children and the people. Our nurse's name was Nhu, which in the native language meant the gentle and peaceful one. The medics and I often spoke about the fact that she was beautiful enough to be in Hollywood or a model. I stayed away from her mostly because I thought she was out of my league, and the unit brass were all around her and keeping her away from us noncoms. She was uniformly polite, gracious, and extremely helpful with the language barriers when we treated the South Vietnamese soldiers. Her gentle style made us think of our girls back home, and we looked forward to just being around her.

One day while we were at Buddha's hooch, Nhu appeared with Captain Willis, our CO (commanding officer). The captain told us that Nhu had heard the *Abbey Road* album that was playing and wanted to join in on the fun to get away from the everyday horrors of war. We were happy to have her and even more happy when Willis left, ignoring the aroma of marijuana, to do his other duties.

Nhu was a Beatles fan just like everybody else. She started to sing along with us. She sat next to me during the sing-a-long where I showed off my entertainer credentials by crooning as smoothly as I could. All the guys lit up joints, and she was amazed that I did not engage in that recreation. She declined an offer to smoke. While the fools I was with drifted into another world instead of attending to this beauty, we sat and talked. There were times during our conversation when I wanted to blurt out that I loved her, but I knew it was because of the loneliness of the situation.

After that day, Nhu and I became great friends. On several movie nights, Nhu would sit next to me, and we would enjoy a night together. The movie which we both enjoyed was *Butch Cassidy and the Sundance Kid* starring Paul Newman, Robert Redford, and the Nhu lookalike, Katherine Ross. Every time I would see a Katherine Ross movie or rerun, I would think of Nhu.

I often daydreamed about her returning with me to the United States so we could bring the relationship up a level. I began feeling better about myself with Nhu around but then she got orders to leave for Da Nang in the North. Her expertise was needed there. I was bereft as she climbed into a chopper with her orders to stay up North until her replacement arrived.

The next day Captain Willis called me to his hooch. He was trembling when he told me her chopper had been shot down before landing in Da Nang and everybody was killed. I was so much in shock I couldn't even cry. I felt numb and in a trance. The only person I had met in "Nam that gave me a reason to live out my tour had been taken away. My days ahead all ran into each other. I had no reason to care what day it was or even if I was going to live another day. I went back to my loneliness.

I had featured that Nhu was heaven sent because while she was there, I received a Dear Jim letter from my girlfriend. I had been dating this beautiful coed, Kathy, who graduated the same year I was supposed to from college. She was then an elementary school teacher. I remembered her empty look when I told her I wasn't quite matriculated yet and now had orders to report to Uncle Sam. She said she'd wait for me. I wanted to believe her so I'd have something to look forward to when my tour was completed.

Because of her, I kept a calendar above my bunk and would cross off a day each morning until the time I would see her again. I wrote her every day, and I waited in the mail call lines one late afternoon, hoping to get a letter from her. Weeks went by without any mail from Kathy. Three weeks went by, and then I got a letter from her. I should have anticipated bad news, given the mail hiatus, but hope springs eternal. I practically snatched the missive from the clerk when my name was called, and I actually was excited. Opening the letter, I spotted "Dear Jim" and thought, "Uh-oh, hope this isn't one of those Dear John letters." It was.

She had met another guy with a great job who was ready to settle down. She didn't want to wait for someone who might never be coming home.

I grabbed the calendar and tore it down. I never paid attention to what date it was again.

CHAPTER 9

BRONZE STAR TIME

When the Vietcong weren't trying to kill us during their five–six mortar attacks per day or through the tactics of using the women who tried to infiltrate the base to finish us off, they decided on another approach, that is, to mount a frontal attack. I was resting in my hooch, watching the reverend praying to several statues, which someone from home had sent him. He had taken to leaving little messages on my bed about being saved by the Lord Jesus Christ now that he knew me a bit better. I felt he really had my best interest at heart. Other than the religious artifacts which he'd receive from time to time, he didn't seem to get much from home. I'd share the goodies I received from my family with him, so we had an interesting truce. My cousin Debby had been a saving grace with her frequent letters filled with news from the states and good humor, which Reverend Randy also relished. He particularly got a kick out of the fact that she called me Squash. It wasn't because I looked like the fruit from the gourd family or even that I knew how to play squash, the racket sport. It was a nickname that followed me throughout my life from age eleven because of a certain incident.

By age eleven, I was almost six feet tall and towered over many of my school chums. I was always chosen first on pick-up games when it came to football and baseball sandlot games. I could run pass and through my friends on the football field and soar over them in basketball.

In retrospect, I played rough in sports and was a showoff. I didn't think I quite deserved a reputation as a little bully, which some of my classmates thought. I hit over twenty homeruns at that age one season and pitched several no-hitters. I'd average fourteen strikeouts a game, and the fathers and older brothers of my victims didn't appreciate my feat. My head was getting sort of big when I would read my name at least once a week in the local newspaper about my prowess on the field. I also maintained all As, so I guess I thought I was the cat's meow.

One day, several older brothers of younger kids I had mowed down at the plate or scored twenty-four points against in basketball asked me to join them in a new game at the local sandpit. To me, I was going to a new level since these were all high school guys. I met them there and was promptly put on the A team to my delight. I was told that this new game was called squash, and that I was an integral part of this game. They directed me to lie on the ground, which I thought was weird, but nonetheless I complied to, so desperate was I for acceptance into the older boys' crowd.

All of a sudden, one by one, they plopped themselves on top of me and squished me into the ground. I was humiliated beyond belief that my high school heroes would do such a thing to me. They laughed as I cried while one of them said, "This is for our little brothers. Have a nice cry."

From that moment on, the name followed me. My cousin Debby would call me that name, no doubt, to exorcize any negative connotation.

I glanced at Reverend Randy while wondering what his world was all about stateside when, all of a sudden, there was a loud crackling noise from outside the hooch. We heard it again as the siren started blaring.

I grabbed my M16 rifle and reached for my M79 grenade launcher. The reverend kept praying and was hesitant to get a weapon. I grabbed him and his rifle as we went outside to gather with the other soldiers at the command post.

"The 'Cong are coming through the wire and attacking with rockets and satchel charges," the sergeant shouted.

On cue, Charlie was filling the air with explosives while charges detonated all over the base. I hadn't handled a weapon since boot camp, so I was a bit insecure. Nonetheless, I sent grenades hurling into the areas designated as enemy territory. I saw hundreds of Vietcong soldiers crawling through the wire, and I thought this would be my last night alive. Literally, hundreds of satchel chargers were thrown in the perimeter, and we suffered many casualties in the firefight. Then I heard noise overhead. Twenty or so helicopters filled the sky and fired multiple rounds from machine guns down at the enemy. Charlie tried to flee to their jungle hideouts, but the firepower cut many of them down as they fled. Another aircraft nicknamed Puff the Magic Dragon came to clean up the attack. That plane had so many weapons that it could cover an area the size of a football field in seconds. The enemy incursion came to an abrupt halt.

Later, we were all presented with Bronze Star Medals. I was proud of the honor and thought that my father would also be impressed. Some of the soldiers, however, tossed their medals away.

There were a lot of injured US soldiers that evening, and I and the medics worked nonstop to save them. The twelve beds in the medical hooch were filled, and as far as I recall, the wounded soldiers all pulled through. There were times, however, when under the rubric of war, where we were supposed to take care of injured enemy soldiers. I remember a time shortly before this attack when we had two Vietcong soldiers in the med hooch. About 3:00 a.m., I went off duty and crawled into bed after a late shift. The station was being manned by two new medic transferees from up north. They had been in intense fighting and were nearing the end of their tour of active combat duty. They had seen a lot of buddies killed by the enemy, and they detested the Vietcong soldiers and sympathizers.

Just as I fell asleep, I heard a loud scream coming from the medical hooch. I feared that harm had come to the transferees. Several of us rushed to help them. One of the transferees was Harlan Bennett, a large-bearded soldier from Alabama. The other new guy was Len Poskli, a Polish American from St. Paul, Minnesota.

Entering the hooch, we spotted both of these men hovering above the beds occupied by the Vietcong soldiers, who were supposed to be guarded by an MP, but who was outside, smoking. They were pouring some kind of solution, later found to be acid, into their wounds. Sergeant Buck Williams, a superior officer who was with us, directed the MP to arrest Bennett and Poskli.

The men were charged with a war atrocity-related crime and transported off the base. The Vietcong soldiers died days later. The camp received no word on what ultimately happened to the two arrested Americans.

On the night of the satchel charge attack, I was glad that no enemy was being attended to in the camp since all hell might have broken loose.

One of the heroes that evening was Johnny Boy. I gave him this nickname since the six foot, blond, blue-eyed soldier looked just like my cousin John, who was at the University of Rhode Island. He was, without a doubt, the most popular man at the aid station together with Buddha. He could get anything on the black market, including women, who loved his looks, to bring back to the base.

He was a cheese-head from Madison Wisconsin so he was a Green Bay Packer's fanatic. One day, we were fed up with the slop that passed for food that we had to eat while officers were dining like kings. So Johnny Boy decided to take matters into his own hands. He had the help of Captain Kelly, our stern company commander who would sometimes look the other way if it raised the morale of the troops. The captain had heard from the company fink, Dave Tuttle, who was back to his old tricks, that we had asked Johnny Boy to get better grub. The captain also yearned for some better food so he ignored the tip from Tuttle.

Johnny Boy headed out in one of the company's trucks and headed off to make some deals. He had some black market movies, flashlights, and Salem cigarettes to trade. The Vietnamese loved the menthol taste and would trade anything for a pack.

Two days went by, and we were fearful that something bad had happened to Johnny Boy. All of a sudden, the truck pulled up, and the back of it was opened. There was a treasure trove of bounty, which included, lobster, steak, shrimp, chicken, watermelon, salad, lamb and beef, and wine and beer. We never asked how he got it all. Ignorance was bliss.

Mission accomplished.

We dined for days on Johnny Boy's stash until it ran out, and we returned to the slop again.

In truth, I figured that Johnny Boy had used his contacts on the black market. Many Americans went home millionaires as a result of the manipulation of such commodities as simple as food. Supply sergeants were able to parlay food destined for soldiers but sold it on the black market instead. Some brass had the equivalent of a diplomatic pouch, so they would buy drugs to ship home to be sold at a later date or bootleg products with channels they controlled.

A key way for making money on the black market was the exchange of military certificates that were used in Vietnam. US soldiers were paid in these certificates, which took the place of greenbacks. Soldiers would have their families send a few hundred dollars. The market would give back three–four times the value of the certificates in return for greenbacks. The GI would offer the money in the black market and would receive $4 of military certificates for that $1 cash. Then the GI would be able to turn back the certificates into dollars by saying his family needed the money, so he'd send the money home with an enhanced value three or four times higher than the pay he initially received in military certificates. After the tour of duty, the soldier could also cash in on the military certificates for George Washingtons.

The black market wanted the American dollar. A lot of this market was controlled by the Vietcong, which was using American money to buy bullets and arms to kill the troops, but greedy soldiers didn't care about that. The Vietcong would get the military certificates to trade by taking them off the bodies of the soldiers they killed when they looted them.

I was tempted a few times to make money that way, but I decided that I didn't want to pay for the bullet that might end my life or that of my buddy. I also felt a bit grossed out by the thought of taking certificates that most often might have been pilfered from soldiers' bodies I might subsequently handle for processing at the aid support station's morgue. Even if I didn't know them personally, I felt a relationship with the deceased.

I considered the military certificates exchanged on the black market to be dirty money in the fullest sense of the term.

CHAPTER 10
A TASTE OF HOME AND LONELINESS

Back at the base camp, my best friend became this little puppy that had wandered into my bunker one evening. I called him Chow, and he was my comforter in the bad times in the war. I took him everywhere. One evening when I was walking him, I became distracted. I couldn't find him. I swear that a mama-san who was working at the base took him, but she denied it. I was forlorn, particularly when I learned that some of the villagers were eating dogs and that young pups were a delicacy for the elders. I tried to make myself believe that he had just run off because the alternative of his being a meal was unthinkable. I could still feel his licking my face. As the time passed, I got very lonely.

My spirits picked up when it was announced that Bob Hope was bringing his show to the base for the troops. I was ecstatic. I bribed an MP to get me in the front row with the hospital patients so I could see real American beauties.

The place went nuts when Bob Hope stepped onto the stage. We all felt that we were back in the good old US of A with nothing to worry about except acne! A group of stars accompanied him. Miss World rocked the place when she stepped into the spotlight. Neil Armstrong, the first man to step on the moon received a hero's welcome. Les Brown and His Band of Renown never sounded better.

Then came the heartthrob of the show, singer Connie Stevens. She reminded us of the girls back home and of our worries as to whether we'd ever see them again (not that I'd be too happy about seeing Kathy after she ditched me!). She was just about ready to launch into the 5th Dimension song "Bill" when she asked if anyone in the front row had that name. I waved my hand.

"Yes!" I shouted.

As far as I was concerned that was my name for the day. Then she called me to the stage. I bounded up the stairs two steps at a time! I shook hands with Mr. Hope and everybody else on stage. It was a thrill meeting Bob Hope and Neil Armstrong and the winner of Miss World, which wasn't exactly a shabby event! Then Connie sang the song to me, and we danced on the platform stage. I was in seventh heaven. I was brought backstage after the serenade to sign a release so the segment could be broadcasted back home in the states.

My segment was seen on advertisements for the show back home although it didn't make the final cut for the telecast. My family at least got a glimpse of me having fun in the promo.

As the show ended, all of us were keyed up with joy until, that is, their plane lifted off. I felt an emptiness inside that was hard to explain, and for a short time, I almost wished they had never come since the touch of home made me and my compatriots more homesick than ever. Drinking the base commissary 3.2 beer didn't help either. The loneliness that ensued among the soldiers was palpable.

My time was coming to a close for that first assignment when something happened that was so funny to me that I was shaken out of my sad reverie. The sirens sounded a couple of days after the show, and we all scampered for cover. I looked in front of me and saw four guys sitting on the latrines trying to get rid of some of that gross army food. All of a sudden, a rocket hit the back of the shitter, and the whole building blew away leaving four embarrassed guys running with their pants around their ankles.

Lai Khe was not the hardest hit area in Vietnam, but I was about to discover some areas that were. My unit, known as the Big Red One, was about to be disbanded. I was called in after three months there to see my commanding officer. He told me that I had been transferred north to the DMZ because of the intense battles going on in the region. He left out the part that the real reason why I was going was because most of the combat medics had been killed or were in dire medical straits.

I was pretty calm. I dreamed that night of a voice in the dark, which was telling me everything would be all right.

The next evening, I said good-bye to my friends at Lai Khe and flew off into the night sky.

"My Dog Chow"
My little buddy who made me happy but
sad when he went away one day.

"Everyone Needs a Friend"
I loved the local children. Most had next to
nothing but they still had a smile to share.

CHAPTER 11
HEADING NORTH

A small army plane was transporting a group of us to the Da Nang airport for our next assignment. I knew I was going to be the medic for a unit but wasn't sure where. I couldn't sleep on the flight. When I was in Lai Khe, I worked with other "docs" and the MDs to patch up soldiers. Now, I was going to be on my own no matter where I'd be assigned. I felt dread at the thought that my knowledge consisted of the films I watched back in boot camp and what I considered silly exercises like stitching two towels together as practice for suturing. My god! I hope nobody got hurt too seriously on my watch. My insecurity grew by the mile as we approached the airport.

Charlie was taking potshots at the plane as we descended toward the airport. A few nicks hit the airplane, but by and large, they were lousy shots, barely grazing the transport. I prayed that their bad aim would persist with the troops with whom I'd be assigned.

At the airport, I stood in line with the other soldiers on my aircraft. Members of the 101st Screaming Eagles were there along with the First Cavalry unit. I chatted with them like a mongoose gone wild since I was frightened by my lack of medic skills, and I was blabbering because of nerves.

When my turn came, I got my orders to report to Dong Ha. A chopper transported me and other soldiers who were assigned to the general area. Needless to say, I was a nonstop chatterbox the closer the chopper got to Dong Ha.

I was processed at the medical command center there and learned that in a few days, I'd be serving at the demilitarized zone in fire support base C. I would be the only medic in this area, replacing six medics who had been killed in action. This wasn't exactly music to my ears. I tried to get some rest, unsuccessfully, until the fated day when the sergeant at Dong Ha pointed to a jeep full of medical supplies and directed me to follow a supply truck headed to the DMZ.

In fact, there was a convoy of trucks bringing supplies to soldiers at various stations along the way. The ride was uneventful through the somewhat mountainous trails. Fortunately, the rainy season was still at least two months away, so none of the vehicles got stuck. As the trip progressed various supply trucks headed down other dirt roads, leaving eventually only me and the one truck I was supposed to follow.

I must have relaxed a little because I was struck by the natural beauty of Vietnam. To me, it had a diverse landscape ranging from high mountains to highlands to tropical islands and river deltas. Vast highland areas also pockmarked the country with forests and waterfalls. Fellow soldiers had told me of the numerous beaches with crystal clear blue-tinted waters from the clear sky. Tropical flowers dotted the landscape and flora and wildlife of many species thrived in that country. How could such a beautiful place be such a hellhole? Something seemed wrong in the scheme of things.

Arriving at the DMZ, the supply truck driver pointed out the medic's bunker. I stepped inside and saw a lot of supplies. I unloaded my jeep with the medical goods I had transported. I was able to stand upright in my dirt bunker. I had one room, about 7' by 6', for sleeping quarters and another room of about the same size where supplies were stored. When I had left the rear base camp, I was given six vials of morphine to use for emergencies. I would soon find out that I'd be offered a king's ransom for the drugs by both sellers and users alike. I put up mosquito netting, carefully tucking it in to the bunk.

Of course, there was a lot of somethings also stored in the bunker, which had been closed up for a while. About every living creature in

'Nam seemed to be living in there. Spiders were as big as my hands, roaches and bugs seemed to have human faces, and there were some species I never had seen before. I tried mightily to evacuate these tenants.

The whole area was weird. When I was walking to the bunker, I could see across the DMZ, which was about two hundred yards wide. The enemy was just right over there. I spotted an elephant, and later I would see an occasional tiger. I turned around to head to my bunker and jumped. A rat about the size of a dachshund ran across the camp and headed into the jungle.

The DMZ ran from east to west, spanning about sixty kilometers. It was the original demarcation between North and South Vietnam as a result of an agreement set at the Geneva Conference back in 1984. Troops from both sides now were supposed to be barred from this area. Howitzers delivered deadly projectiles from the north, making the concept of a nonaggression zone a joke. At any time, without warning, a barrage of incoming rounds could strike, leaving destruction and carnage in its wake. Various soldier companies were stationed along the DMZ.

I decided to meet my immediate neighbors, who were the soldiers that I would be spending my time with most during that tour. They were the mine sweepers (sweeps) and an armored carrier group. Their job was to go out at 4:30 a.m. or 5:00 a.m. each morning and sweep the DMZ to search for land mines. The enemy would make nightly excursions more often than not and under cover of darkness to plant mines. The protocol was for neither camp to breach the DMZ. This was mostly honored by our troops unless there was a firefight instigated by the Vietcong and we retaliated in defense. The enemy troops took every opportunity to ignore the rules.

I slightly knocked on the door leading to the bunker of the sweeps. I heard loud music from a Jimi Hendrix record, so I figured they couldn't hear me. I opened the makeshift door and walked down about a half-dozen steps.

The bunker was filled with smoke from the bongs the soldiers were sucking. The music was extremely loud. A string of purple lights was stretched horizontally between two walls and gave off a violet haze. The rest of the bunker was dark. About twenty-four guys inhabited this huge bunker as far as I could make out. Two mama-sans were waiting to be summoned for sex duty.

I shouted a greeting to the men, who then looked at me. When I announced I was the new doc, the name given to medics in 'Nam, there were quite a few huzzahs! Master Sergeant John Mayo approached me and gave me a bear hug that lifted me off my feet.

"Glad to see you, Doc!"

He continued to tell me that the men had lost a beloved medic named Billy Sherman. He had lost his life in the line of duty. Sherman not only took great care of the health of his men but always went on patrols with as many units that wanted a morale boost by having a medic nearby.

"Billy was also a fierce fighter. He mixed it up with the best of them. Besides his medical bag, he carried an M16 rifle, two handguns, and grenades."

His voice became quiet. One day on patrol, Billy's unit was ambushed near a ravine in the bush. Several men were killed and many more injured, including Billy. With a severely injured leg wound, he crawled to help his unit while putting himself further in harm's way. He took several shots to the torso. While administering to the wounded, Medevac choppers came to the rescue, and the men that Billy had treated survived and lived to tell the story. Billy Sherman died that day a hero.

I resolved that very moment that I'd go out on every assignment as well. I needed to get more firepower though other than my M16.

I started to shake hands with some of the men. Several soldiers were wearing some necklaces which at first I thought were unusual charms around their necks. As they came closer into view I saw that they had neckwear that was made of human ears. It seemed that the thing to do was not only to kill the enemy but to chop off an ear in order to display your fighting prowess. I felt like I was going to regurgitate but got my stomach under control.

"New Condo Up For Sale Real Cheap"
My Home at the DMZ loaded with every living thing you can imagine.

"Chippendales on the DMZ"
That's me with the DMZ in the background. During
the day you could see the North Vietnamese moving
ammo and troops into areas around the perimeter.

CHAPTER 12

SPIRITS COME VISITING

One day on patrol in the jungle, we arrived at an area where no GI had apparently gone before. I was walking just behind the radio operator when, all of a sudden, I saw some movement in the trees just ahead and to the right of me. No one else seemed to see or hear anything. Then this shadowy figure appeared on a large branch on a tree on the side of the right path. Our point man was leading to the left, and the figure pointed to the right. I yelled back to the pack to halt, and when I looked for the figure, it was nowhere in sight. I called for our point man to search inch by inch on the left side path. He uncovered a slew of trip wires hooked to explosives on the trail where the image had told me not to walk.

Shortly thereafter, I was driving a jeep with wounded soldiers who needed a MASH unit attention in the rear of our fire support unit. As I drove through a deserted village area, I saw the figure again telling me to turn right and not go straight. I instinctively obeyed and floored the vehicle to the right. As I took off and six to eight Vietcong came out of the ground and commenced shooting at us in the jeep. I could hear the *rat tat tat* of the bullets bouncing off the vehicle. If I had gone straight, we all would have been blown away.

The phrase "spider hole" refers to a hole in the earth, often used by the enemy for a sneak attack. The Vietcong in Vietnam had an extensive network of tunnels. This experience and others taught me and my comrades in arms to dread the specter of enemy soldiers popping out of these small holes. Each was covered by camouflaged lids at ground level. Often, they were six–eight feet long and allowed enough room for a person to lie down. These holes were not only used for sniper attacks but also to give warning to patrols that there were incoming American troops.

As I escaped, I looked to the skies to see if I had been sent a guardian angel.

Some men might write it off to the fact that maybe drugs were influencing me, but I hadn't taken any, including the J. Maybe, it was a lack of sleep, which was plausible. I decided to just file the incidences in my memory bank.

Subsequent events would challenge my thinking that these were explainable events with an earthly reason. There was one man, however, who was an earthly angel to me and a lot of us. His name was An Dung, which translates to "peaceful hero" in Vietnamese. He was part of the South Vietnamese army and trained by his country and by the United States Special Forces. He was only five feet tall but ruggedly built and was an expert in martial arts. He specialized in finding and destroying spider holes. I, and most of us, could not spot these holes beforehand with our naked eyes, but An Dung knew all the signs of one of these being close by. We got to be good friends, and I learned a lot about the Vietnamese people from him. After a patrol together, we would sit down and swig a few beers and talk about our families and what it would mean to be free from the North Vietnam regime.

There would be many times that An Dung would find and destroy these spider holes, thus allowing us to move forward on patrol. He was assigned to several units, so when he wasn't with mine, I'd say a prayer for his safety. Word came back one day that he had been trying to clear out one spider hole when he was killed. He had crawled halfway down a hole and got stuck while trying to clear it. He was shot several times but managed to drop a grenade down the hole. He had removed the danger to his unit. Another true hero of that war was gone.

The only funerals I attended were for South Vietnamese soldiers although I mourned all my comrades' deaths. I went to An Dung's. A Vietnamese proverb says, "The sense of the dead is that of the final," implying that funeral ceremonies must be solemnly organized. As sad as any funeral is, a Vietnamese funeral is heartwarming.

At the funeral, the body is washed and dressed. A chopstick is laid between the teeth and then a pinch of rice and three coins are dropped in the mouth. The body is laid on a grass mat spread on the ground and enveloped in a white cloth. It then is placed in a coffin. Finally, the funeral service is performed. The coffin is buried, but after three days of mourning, the family visits the tomb and opens the grave again for worship. Finally, after forty-nine days, the family stops bringing rice to the dead at the altar. At the one-hundred-day mark, the family celebrates Tot Khoc, or the end of tears. After one year, there is a ceremony for the first anniversary of the relative's death, and after two years, a festival ensues to mark the end of the mourning period.

The customs of the Vietnamese people is one of respect for tradition. In An Dung's funeral, I periodically appeared when I could as my duties allowed. I also attended several other funerals of my South Vietnam comrades, but it wasn't too long before I reverted back to my own problems of survival. But as I learned to live with death, I gradually became numb to my surroundings.

CHAPTER 13
BEING A REAL MEDIC

Being the company medic made me rue the day that I'd have some serious patch-up work to do. One day while I was on the perimeter with some troops, an American soldier came walking out of the jungle, holding something in his hand. As he got closer, I saw it was one of his ears that had been severed from his head.

"Doc, put this back on. I'm in a hurry."

As I looked at him and his ear, all I could think of was sewing the two towels back in Fort Sam Houston. I froze for a moment but shook off my nerves. He put his ear next to his face where it was missing. This guy was about 6'5", weighed about 300 lbs., and was high as a kite.

"Yes, keep that ear right where you've got it," I said with some authority which I didn't feel. I sutured it back in place.

"Thanks, Doc." He walked off. I was glad that he didn't have a mirror.

He made me feel good and needed. To this day, I know that he is walking around with the most crooked ear around and probably looking for the doc who did it.

Another GI came to my bunker with a gunshot wound to the leg. With the help of his buddy who brought him to me, we tied off an artery to stop the bleeding and got him evacuated to a hospital all the way back to Da Nang. He said thanks and gave me a homemade knife, which I still treasure to this day. That time I did well. I was beginning to think that I maybe wasn't too awful a medic.

I was certainly getting on the job training, but my sarge had me earmarked for bigger and riskier jobs, and he turned out to be the guy who could teach me.

Master Sergeant Mayo knew *everything*, and I mean everything. He was a lifer, which was the term for the full-timers in the military. His body was lean and mean, and he looked like he was genetically engineered for this kind of war. He was skilled as any medic would be although he didn't have the title. He had seen every wound available and dressed or handled it when no medics were around. It actually was him who taught me the formula to avoid VD by pouring whiskey over the genital area and squeezing at least a few drops of urine to kill any disease.

I became a really good medic under his tutelage. That did not to mean I didn't make stupid mistakes. Take Jamie, a grunt, who came to my bunker sporting about forty stitches and asked me to take them out. I said sure and proceeded to remove them. My medical training at San Antonio had never showed us how to remove stitches, but I thought that was because it was such an easy and mundane task. I couldn't figure it out while loads of blood was oozing from each suture.

"Doc, what the hell is this?" he asked with a worried voice.

I told him this was normal and it would heal by itself. He was actually stifling shouts of pain during the time I was removing them.

I wrapped him up and sent him on his way. I decided to check with Master Sergeant Mayo. After I recounted the story, he asked, "Did you cut the knots first?"

I could never face Jamie again. Fortunately for me, he was goofed up on so many self-administered drugs, he couldn't feel pain for very long.

I hung out with the master sergeant every time we went out. He patiently instructed me, usually with a nod or a cough rather than with words so he wouldn't undermine my "skills" before the men. Soon, he didn't have to do anything anymore. He had turned me into a confident medic.

"Nowhere to Hide"
Vietnamese women and children forced to leave
their homes. Most never came back.

CHAPTER 14

THE MOD SQUAD AND OTHER CHARACTERS

Dave Lorins was one of the guys living in the large bunker next to mine. He was a good ole boy from Montana. He drove a tank. Besides heading out to the perimeter to scout for land mines, his team also searched for land mines used to disrupt the supply lines. I belatedly thanked them for keeping me safe en route to fire support base C when I first arrived there.

On one such excursion, we heard on the radio that a local village was about to be ravaged by the North Vietnamese troops. They were en route to loot the town and rape the women. We headed to the village because the inhabitants had been friendly to us. Theoretically, the enemy was not supposed to be in this South Vietnam zone because of the Geneva Convention, but obviously, they could care less about such niceties.

Upon arrival, we slowed down and spotted about two dozen North Vietnamese soldiers heading toward the village. We fired on them. They scattered and ran back to the north. The villagers were grateful that we interceded, and much later, they would tell us of enemy troop movements into our territory in order to show their gratitude.

While it was not the rainy season, in the DMZ, when it rained, it poured. Everything was flooded and more and more I was knee deep in water, which made things hard to accomplish. It somewhat dampened the enemy's attacks as well. I still got patients, but sometimes, the injured men were shot by friendly fire. I wondered how much being high had contributed to the injuries done to these men by their fellow soldiers.

One disturbing incident involved a 2nd Lt. Donald Peterson. Lieutenants like him were usually fresh from officer's candidate schools or from one of the academies like West Point. Book knowledge differed from reality, so some of them led their patrols into areas where only the enemy was to be or else got them lost in the jungle. That led to an across-the-board scorn from the noncommissioned soldiers. Some of the lieutenants demanded discipline. Apparently, that was Lieutenant Peterson's crime. He died at the support base. I noticed that his bullet wound came from an army weapon.

As the helicopter evacuated him, I started to develop a slight twitch and ringing in my ears. Soon, I was shaking something fierce when I heard an evac helicopter since I knew what they were carrying. At night, I would see the wounded or dead soldiers in my sleep, and I would awaken in a huge sweat. During the day though, I managed to hold it together. I told nobody about these problems since it would be disheartening for the men to think their medic had issues.

One guy who came new to camp was Rafer "Lightning" Harris, who was a piece of work. The soldiers called him Lightning because it took him two days to do an hour's work. He worked out on weights every day; was built like Lawrence Taylor, the New York Giants linebacker; loved the Vietnam women; and drank some fine wine, which he'd purchase from the black market when he went back to Da Nang.

We used to drive to the rear villages together to bring back some entertaining young ladies for games and fun. Lightening was always the life of the party. He never bugged me for meds as some soldiers did. I never gave up morphine regardless of the pleas by anyone not needing it for an injury.

One day, he came to my bunker with blood gushing from his genital area and screaming at the top of his lungs. I gave him a pain shot and laid him on the table to take a look. His whole groin area was ripped apart and shredded like lettuce. It seemed that Rafer had gone with another soldier to another village and latched on to a Vietcong princess, who had been fixed with a razor blade inside her vagina. And when Lightning struck, he was ripped.

We had been warned about such incidences but never thought it would happen to any of us. Rafer got to go home, and I heard that they fixed him up somewhat so he could operate as a man back in the states.

Another character on the base was Luke Flynn. He didn't seem to belong to any platoon, and nobody cared to check where he was supposed to be. He came in for a VD shot a couple of times, and we struck up a friendship. He took me to his abode, which was hidden away in a rear area not traveled by many. There stood a creepy little shack that looked like a fall-out shelter that had been hit with grenades a few times. On the inside, the walls were covered with all sorts of firearms from German Lugers to large or small machine guns. In another room were two hooch maids who catered to his every need. He opened up a small chest, and it had weed from many different countries like Cambodia, Thailand, Algeria, and Bangladesh to name a few. He offered me a few Js, but I told him I didn't smoke. He called in the girls, who smoked the Js to their heart's content. They really seemed not to notice me.

Later, I asked him what division he was in, and I learned that he was a deserter. He had been living there for about a year, and nobody came looking for him. It seemed that they had him missing in action, and that was fine with him. He wanted to take the time to decide if he wanted to stay in Vietnam.

I asked him if people at the base knew his status. He said yes, but that nobody cared. In fact, he told me that he had sold marijuana and guns to soldiers and officers alike. He also dealt with the locals, and his collection of weapons was outstanding. He would trade everything from cigarettes to medical supplies, which he acquired by any means possible. I sort of surreptitiously looked him over to see if he had taken anything from my bunker, but it appeared he had not.

He asked me not to make any report on him. When I agreed (and why I did I'm still not sure), he brought a present for me to take back to the home base. Rolled up in a white sheepskin were two pearl-handled, snub-nosed .38s with a holster that looked like they were just shipped in from the manufacturer. I was excited about my gift and put them around my waist, and that seemed to lift his spirits. As I left his hideaway, he threw a German Lugar at me and said, "Here's one for the road."

I was now feeling more like my predecessor, Medic Billy Sherman, since I'd be armed to the teeth, and half-wondered whether his guns had come from Flynn.

I didn't see Flynn for a while. Then a report came in that his shack had been satchel charged. I never heard from him again. Perhaps he is still in Vietnam and planned the whole disappearing act himself. I could only hope that he was okay.

Homesickness continued to plague all of us no matter how tough we appeared to be. On one of my visits back to the rear to secure medical supplies, I noticed that the officer's club had pizza parties several nights a week. Being a noncom, I never was invited, but the cooks had mercy on me and would give me several slices. As I passed by the club, I looked in the window and saw officers and nurses partying to their heart's content. Thinking about my comrades eating junk mostly out of cans, I concocted a scheme on the spot.

With my visits I had learned that during the day, there were certain times when the officer's mess was empty. Absolutely nobody was around during this window of opportunity. I sneaked into the mess with four of my comrades from the fire base, unplugged the pizza oven, and carried it out to our truck. We loaded tons of pizza dough, tomatoes, and cheese. Because I was driving a medical truck, we breezed through the gate without any inspection.

Life was good! The pizzas were great. Best of all, we never got caught.

Finally, I got a call from the rear telling me that I had been in Vietnam enough of days to earn some R & R in the country for a week. I was going on vacation!

"Mod Squad"
Named after the popular TV series these guys helped
patrol the DMZ and keep the perimeters safe.

CHAPTER 15

FINALLY, SOME R & R

I was offered a choice between Thailand and Hawaii for my week of vacation. I went off to Honolulu without a moment's hesitation. I had about $200 from changing my military certificates for cash. I had hoped I would have had more money, but the nightly poker games and partying with girls had depleted my account. I was raring to go! I was hoping that my symptoms would disappear as soon as I got some rest.

I was set up by the army in a nice hotel near Waikiki Beach that was crowded with prostitutes from the mainland, trying to sell their wares to GIs who hadn't seen round-eyed women in months and who would pay big bucks for a night of entertainment. I decided to work another deal where I'd meet beautiful ladies without spending any money.

I began by surveying the whole island and learning where the tourist traps were and set myself up like Jim Dye, the Hawaiian-born tour guide. I already had a rich dark tan from Vietnam, and my hair was now long enough, so I could pass for anything from an Arab to an Italian stallion. Hair length no longer was an issue in the jungle, so I looked like a civilian. I watched buses letting off tourists at several hotels and waited to talk to them outside. I offered my newly learned tourist services to several busloads but got no buyers.

Then a busload of school teachers from Oklahoma pulled up to the curbing, and I set my eyes on a pretty lady in the front seat who happened to be the team leader from the school. I gave her every line I could muster, and she hired me to take the forty teachers around the mainland the next day. They had rented a bus for the week and were actually looking for a guide. God, I couldn't believe my luck!

I told her that I worked on a tip basis only, and I took her to dinner to seal the deal. Her name was Becky Hollis, and she was a homespun gal and a little naive to say the least. She believed all the stories I told her about my life in Hawaii and about my being abandoned by my family and living off the land. We had a great time talking and dancing the night away, and I was ready for my first tour.

I brought the teachers to most of the tourist traps on the main island, and yes, even to see Don Ho. I was tipped around $100 by the ladies for the day and continued to see Becky while she was there. When she left, I took her phone number, but we both knew that we'd never speak to each other again.

I spent the next few days feeling homesick and called home to talk to some familiar voices. I stayed fourteen days and was AWOL when I finally returned back to combat. I was given an Article 15 and the punishment was a month's lost wages.

I was now back to the same old grind of mine patrol and patching up the guys. We were on patrol, and again I experienced a voice telling me to stay away from the left path. I called up to the point man, and he carefully checked the path. There was a well-disguised hole that had punji stakes. The Vietcong would often plant these sharpened sticks and cover them with poison and feces. The unsuspecting soldier would step on them, and these would pierce the boots and feet, so sharp were they. Illness would set in fairly quickly, and sometimes death occurred.

The ringing in my ears returned as well as an annoying twitch, which would make people think that I had a severe physical disorder. Nobody on my team ever asked me about it because they probably were too stoned most of the time to recognize it.

Several days after the punji incident, I received a visit from one of the friendly village leaders, who said that one of the mothers was in trouble trying to deliver her baby. I had no training in delivering babies, but it was not a good thing to turn down any request from the home folk there. They could be your best friend or your worst enemy, to borrow the phrase, and I knew I had to help. I at first called back to the rear to find if somebody more competent than me was available. There wasn't anyone. In fact, the person who answered was rude, quipping, "Who cares if another gook is born."

I asked to speak to a nurse who helped me with instructions. When I arrived at the village, the entire population was outside her hut. As I entered, I could see that the mother was in tremendous pain. It seemed as though the baby was stuck, and she could not push the bambino loose from its nine-month home.

With hands sweaty from nerves, I used the information the nurse gave me to help widen the area of delivery and to turn the baby slightly around, so it could come out easier. The village women gave a sigh, which sounded good, and then they took over. They actually did the tough work, but they treated me like I had magic hands that made everything come out well

I was a hero, so over the next few months, they came for me to supervise five more births.

My reward for that tough pregnancy was that the villagers would not tell the North Vietnamese soldiers any of our positions in the field. But that wasn't all. After the first difficult birth, I was also the guest of honor at a dinner with the village chief leaders.

My CO authorized me to go to the sit-down dinner. He actually told me to eat and enjoy everything since whatever they served. It would be considered insulting not to eat it. I felt as though I was on a diplomatic mission.

My imagination was working overtime as to what the hell I'd be putting in my tummy since the CO had sort of a smirk on his face when he was reminding me of my manners. He added that it would be like another R & R event, which I richly deserved. His double meaning was not lost on me.

The entire village stood outside the head chief's hut as I entered it and sat down at a table with the elders, their wives, and their eligible daughters. After a long ceremony and prayer session, course number one was served. It was a large egg with an unusual smell to it. A small straw poked out of it. I was asked to be the first to taste it because I was the honored guest. As I sucked in the egg accompanied by nodding heads of approval, I remembered my CO's order to eat everything or I would insult the whole village. My stomach began to churn as the rotten egg went down my throat. This little delicacy had been buried in the ground for one hundred days and had gotten a little ripe, to say the least, but this was the best part of the meal. The next course was a whole fish, which had to be eaten, gills and all. This fish as well had been baked in the sun for weeks. Everybody at the table looked at me to make sure I was enjoying it. I smiled at them with an assurance that I didn't have. I was about to blow up the food in one hurl when the main course arrived. In Vietnam, the head of anything was the best meal to be served. In front of me were ten chicken heads with their eyeballs looking at me and their beaks glistening. Everyone at the table except me was wishing they could have had those heads to eat. All they had was the breasts and legs to eat. What a shame. I picked at the heads, drank some wild nectar, and couldn't wait to get out of there.

The chief offered me one of the eligible women for a nightcap. I was afraid that I'd throw up on her, so I took a raincheck on the girl and got the hell out of there. On the way home, I stopped five times to vomit. I didn't eat anything for two days. I was, however, respected for my heroics by both the villagers and my CO. I only hoped that I would not receive any more dining invitations.

CHAPTER 16

LOVE AT FIRST SIGHT

Armed with my two pearl-handled firearms and the German Luger and my medical gear, I went out on patrol with the soldiers. We came upon a village that had been recently hit by airstrikes. Everywhere I looked, there were mama-sans crying for their dead relatives. Villagers who were missing limbs abounded. When I first came into this country, seeing a scene like this would make me teary-eyed. Now, all I felt was numbness. I wasn't happy that my heart was now made of stone and that all I could think about was myself and how soon I would get out of that place.

I tried helping them with medical supplies like bandages, ointment, etc., but my comrades in arms didn't look too kindly on my helping these people. I called for more support from the rear to help clean up the mess, again an action that didn't endear me to the guys with whom I was patrolling.

The soldiers confiscated ammo and weapons in order to ensure that patrols after us would find the area clear of danger.

Along the way, we often paused while guys would be with a young girl for his needs in exchange for a pack of cigarettes or a can of food rations. The whole setup was unfortunate since the gals were no older than twelve and in an unequal bargaining position. Their families would send them out for food and small amounts of money, so all of them could live another day.

Pregnancies resulted from these liaisons. It was pretty well documented that thousands of babies were Asian American, and at that time, these children were outcasts since their own country would not recognize them as citizens. To this day, I wonder if all these poor sons and daughters of GIs (including maybe my own) survived the war. For most of us, the sex was a one-night stand and anonymous.

Some men were involved in a steady relationship, thinking that they had fallen in love. Whether it was reciprocal or not was hard to determine since the Vietnamese woman certainly wanted a ticket out of the ravages of war. They would also be ostracized if they looked pro-American. It was a far better cultural advantage to have sex with a GI to support your extended family, given the hardship of daily life versus falling in love with the devil.

My platoon mate, Dave Lorins, actually fell in love and asked me to be his best man at the wedding in the girl's village. I really struggled with his request. I was honored to be asked, but I really didn't believe in these marriages, given the entirety of the circumstances. I declined. I didn't have to tender a reason because he did not ask for one. I believe he understood that I was skeptical of such marriages under the trying circumstances of loneliness and, yes, if I am honest, security reasons. I wasn't totally convinced that the enemy wouldn't be exported state side though these marriages.

His bride was part French and Asian and had exotic features. I hoped for the best, including the fact that I prayed that the nuptials wouldn't just be a free ride for her to the states.

The military service was just as concerned as I personally was about these marriages. It took usually over a year for the okay to be given for a Vietnamese bride to go to the United States. Often, the soldier would return home first and wait for the bride he married in Vietnam. I subsequently learned that Dave first left Vietnam, and his wife was given the okay to join him. I believe they live in Indiana now.

Some GIs also bit the dust with Vietnamese women. Knowing the red tape, they would go AWOL and disappear into the bush without ever being seen again.

I was very confused by the entire sexual liaisons in Vietnam, including taking responsibility for one's actions. My conscience, however, was short-lived when it came to my needs.

One day before his marriage, I took Dave with me to the rear to pick up some medical supplies we needed at our compound. We took an alternate route since we had heard from command that there was some fire action along the usual route to the supply depot.

As we navigated the twists and turns over several hills and valleys, we came upon a bunker with several army vehicles surrounding it. There were at least twenty-five GIs standing outside waiting to get into the site. Dave and I figured there was probably food for rationing being passed out to these grunts in the field. We also noticed that they were leaving their weapons outside the bunker.

A Red Cross truck was parked in the back, so we continued to surmise that the organization had sent pizza, donuts, and packages for the weary soldiers, which was the organization's wont.

"Dave, let's get in line and see what they brought."

The Red Cross workers were all American, so I figured seeing them could make me less homesick.

There wasn't much conversation in line, but we observed that when each GI got closer to the entrance, they appeared to be giving money to two large men on each side. I asked an army corporal what the money was for, and he said it was for the Donut Dolly's. I must have looked perplexed because he added, "You know, the round-eyed women."

When we got to the entrance, the robust guys asked what we wanted and cited prices for various services inside the bunker. The so-called Red Cross girls were actually prostitutes from mainland Hawaii, who knew that the guys were lonely for American ladies and took advantage of this fact with high-priced services.

Most of the men had paid several hundred dollars, apparently as per the prices cited to us. Dave and I had no money, so we were asked to leave. I probably would have paid the scratch for the company of a round eye. I'm sure the young ladies were making a lot of money, and Dave and I discussed whom we thought had authorized them to come into the country. It had to be approved by some higher-up.

After picking up the supplies, we headed back to our bunker a bit frustrated until we saw our mama-sans waiting to service us.

CHAPTER 17

ANOTHER KIND OF PREJUDICE

It was a gloomy day at the fire support base. One of the armored carrier grunts woke me to check out a wounded GI lying in a bunker across from the DMZ. I rushed to the scene and was horrified to see a young recruit's body pressed up against sandbags on the side of the bunker. I couldn't recognize his face since profuse bleeding still ran over his head from a severe beating he must have gotten just minutes before I saw him. He was barely breathing, and I used all the medical training I knew to stabilize him. As I gingerly cleaned his face, I realized it was Timothy, our beloved cook.

Two months earlier, Timothy Rogan, a young, handsome recruit form Southern California, had sought for a new chapter in his life and enlisted in the army. He had big dreams of learning a trade in the service and starting his own business someday. He always loved cooking, and the thought of him becoming a master chef someday gave him a positive outlook for the future. His first step was joining the local National Guard as a cook. It was working out well for this weekend warrior until his unit was called up for combat, a rarity in those days.

Timothy arrived in Da Nang to be processed out to a unit in need of his MOS as a cook. It was coincidence that our own cook there at C2 had just finished his tour and was on his way home to the states.

Timothy got his orders to join us on the DMZ, and he hopped on the first chopper heading our way.

We couldn't believe our luck when he arrived. We were excited that finally we had someone who could mix and match the crap that the military gave us to eat and could turn it not only into something edible but gourmet! Everybody in the unit took a shine to this likable kid, especially Sergeant Lodi, who kind of took Timothy under his wing. Lodi drilled Timothy on all the survival tactics to keep him safe, and he seemed to enjoy the other's company.

I thought it somewhat strange that every time we had a party with the local village girls, Timothy was in absentia. I chalked it up to his shyness. Nobody else seemed to notice his absence from our hooch get-togethers.

Timothy was also loved by the local villagers. He would make extra food for the guys and deliver the remaining portion to the poor souls in the village. The children always looked forward to the candy he'd scrounge together for them.

Just before I found Timothy akimbo, I was awakened by some loud voices coming from the 101st bunker across the camp. I popped my head out just in time to see Timothy running away and sobbing. I didn't think too much about it at the time, and the next morning, I was called back to the MASH unit to pick up supplies. That was the last time I saw Timothy before returning and finding him beaten and bleeding.

As was protocol, I needed to put together a report about this cruel incident. Nobody knew anything. I called in Sergeant Lodi, figuring that I could get a straight story from this best friend. Lodi was tight-lipped. I told him that I had to get a full report back to HQ (headquarters), and if I didn't get the right facts together, that there most likely would be a full-blown investigation.

"Heads could roll," I told Lodi.

We sat down overlooking the DMZ, and with tears in his eyes, Sergeant Lodi started to speak.

"You know, Timothy and I were tight. I loved the little guy, and we had a lot in common except one thing." His pause lasted a near eternity.

"The night you saw him running from the bunker sealed his doom. We were celebrating a successful combat mission in our bunker with local girls, booze, and of course, some awesome weed. It was the first party that Tim had ever come to, so the guys were trying to make it memorable for him. They watched him down several pitchers of beer and gave him some lively brownies so he'd have something in his stomach. Those brownies really had an effect on him and turned Tim into another personality." He paused again to regain his composure.

"Tim started dancing around and singing weird songs. Finally, he sat down in the corner next to Troy Bennett, that handsome surfer dude from Miami. The party was going strong until Troy suddenly stood up and punched Timothy in the face. Tim's nose was bleeding, and he raced out of the bunker, sobbing. That's when you saw him that night."

Lodi continued. "We grabbed Troy and held him down, wondering why he would pop such a beloved guy like Tim. We didn't expect the answer we were given.

'Let me up,' Troy shouted as we were about to put a hurt on him for ruining the party.

'You guys, are not going to believe this, but your buddy Timothy tried to put the moves on me. He asked me if I had ever been with another man, and he grabbed my crotch. He said he had been eyeing me all night and that he had a good insight into gay men. That's when I let him have it. I'm not going to have a fag loose at my party, and for sure, we don't want him around in this camp."

Lodi told me that the rest of the men all grunted in the affirmative and went back to drinking and smoking weed. As the evening wore on, Troy started instigating a lynch mob to teach the fag a lesson.

"Five of us left the party in the wee hours of the morning and went to Tim's bunker. I stood at the door and watched Troy and the others put a sheet over Tim's head, at which time they took turns beating and kicking him over and over again. Tim was my best friend, but I couldn't let the others think that I was protecting a homo. Like a coward, I watched, and I will not forget what I did not do to try to stop it. I just didn't want them suspecting me of being a switch-hitter. We dumped him in the bunker where you found him hours later. I didn't even come to you to help him."

Lodi walked away in despair with his head hanging low.

I was sick. I wondered about what other problems could occur because somebody was different—maybe religious beliefs or none thereof? Male versus female? There was a war within a war. What was disheartening for me was that Sergeant Lodi had been a multi-decorated soldier who didn't have the guts to stand up to the others. I thought it quite ironic that he taught survival skills to Timothy so he'd protect himself against the enemy when the enemy turned out to be within.

I sent my report, the unadulterated facts, to HQ; and for some reason, it got lost along the way. I thought, "What else is new?" Soldier upon soldier fighting based on prejudice was normally covered up. These kinds of problems were swept under the rug.

Timothy recovered physically, but mentally, he wasn't the same man who entered the base. He was sent back to the United States labeled "unfit to be in combat."

To this day, I hope he did well. I miss his cooking. I miss him.

CHAPTER 18

SELF-INFLICTED WOUNDS

While at Dong Ha, I was also surprised as to how many soldiers I had to try to patch up there were. They needed my services because they inflicted their own wounds to get out. Some GIs had stepped out the door through desertion, many of whom had fled to the highlands. Others whom I treated went all out, filling themselves with drugs so as to render themselves unfit for duty. Their game was to get sent to rehabilitation facilities and off the battlefield. Then there was this as just one example.

I was returning back from the latrine when I heard a loud bang and a scream. I rushed over to the spot. Lying there was Big John Tracey, who was about 6'4" and weighed about 260 lbs. He hated authority and swore to the troops that his stay in 'Nam wouldn't be very long. He tried every scheme in the book, and now had resorted to shooting himself in one of his legs. I looked at this wound, and it was huge. He swore it was an accident caused by cleaning his gun, but I could see that it wasn't. He was a left-handed so the wound was in the right leg. Dirt was kicked up into the wound, causing contamination. He was bleeding profusely, and I stopped most of it with a makeshift tourniquet. I enlisted assistance to transport him to the MASH tent, so an army doctor could work on him.

The doctor shook his head in disgust as he extracted the bullet. In the end, Big John got what he wanted, a ticket out the door, but it got punched with the loss of his right leg, which couldn't be saved. Variations of lower extremity self-injury included a shot to the foot. Since most GIs were right-handed, an injury to the second toe of the left foot was suspicious.

Sometimes I treated self-inflicted (or buddy-inflicted) wounds to the hand. These were usually more severe to treat, so the soldier was usually sent home

In the field, many other soldiers either plugged themselves or had their buddies do it with enemy weapons that the troops had confiscated in order to get out of the war.

Theoretically, the service considered self-inflicted wounds to be a serious military offense. Nobody, to my knowledge, got prosecuted. I'm not sure what the MASH doctor reported on Tracey. We medics were reluctant to blow the whistle on anyone and so were the medical doctors since some injuries were susceptible to a conclusion that it was an accident. There also was an attitude that there was a mental condition, if someone injured himself so that hook led to no prosecution as I could tell.

I used to talk a lot about getting out but didn't have the guts to get out this way.

CHAPTER 19

MORE CARNAGE AND TROUBLE

As per the usual routine, we boarded armored vehicles in the early morning and proceeded to patrol the perimeter and check for land mines on the DMZ. We moved through the jungle terrain on one of these carriers. The guys were relaxed with the usual J hanging from their mouths. All of a sudden, the old voice in my head kept saying to get off the carrier. Without questioning what was going on, I jumped to another carrier and started to tell the other guys to jump off the first carrier. A loud explosion interrupted my admonition. That carrier I was on had hit a land mine, which exploded up through the bottom. The screams inside the tank turned to silence.

As the medic, I rushed to see if there was anything I could do. As I approached with a heavy heart, I saw pieces of the vehicle all over the place. Looking inside, I saw parts of bodies, but one GI was still alive and pressed against one of the walls of the carrier. I got to him and patched him up with the limited medical supplies I had and called in a medical evac 'copter to take him to the rear.

As soon as he was taken away, the unit continued to secure the area for more mines. I couldn't help but wonder about the voice saving me. The ride back was pretty somber with guys, no doubt, wondering when it would be their turn to go back in a body bag.

We would have many more missions along the DMZ and would never know when something bad would happen.

I thought it was coincidental, but I noticed that I was having more and more difficulty breathing. I spoke to my sergeant who was safely encamped back in the rear. He and I never got along. He was a real spit-and-polish man, and I was somebody just trying to put in my time and get the hell out of there alive. When I told him of my breathing problem, he ragged on me, calling me a coward. He told me he'd give me another assignment all right, but it would be to a support base where I was guaranteed to leave in a body bag.

Since I pretty much was on my own, I took a chopper to Da Nang to visit the MASH unit there, after getting permission from my top CO to do so. I arrived at night and saw several officer parties underway all over the place. Noncom grunts like me were left to fend for themselves, so I joined a gang at the local watering hole. It was full of ladies of the night, looking for some GI dough. My sinus condition was so bad, I passed up the opportunity for their services and returned very early to my bunk.

The next morning, I saw a doctor. While waiting for him, I was impressed by the commitment of the nurses and doctors around me. They were doing a bang-up job of tending to the wounded. Dr. Burrows came in an introduced himself. We discussed hometowns and family while I went through some testing. He came back with the proverbial good news and bad news. The bad news flash was that I had rhinitis, an inflammation of the nasal mucous membrane caused by an allergic reaction to the plant life in the northern regions of 'Nam. I smiled when he told me that he was going to get me a transfer back to the rear in the south of Vietnam (the good news!). He wrote up the orders and said it would take a couple of weeks to put all the paperwork together.

I flew back with my new orders and presented them to my cranky sergeant. After calling me a lot of really nice names, he assigned me to the rear to await my evacuation south. Three weeks later, I still hadn't received the transport order. Sarge, with a smirk of delight, was about to send me back out into the bush. Just as I was packing to return to the field, the orders arrived, and I took the first chopper out and waved good-bye to the DMZ and my knucklehead sarge.

I was flown to Long Binh where I would meet John Banner and Phil Fournier. They would become my good friends over my remaining time. We would share some interesting adventures while we waited for the big bird to take us back home.

We got along with almost everybody because we were medics, and everyone wanted us to be there for them if they got wounded or needed a shot of penicillin after playing with the village girls. John was a well-educated Southerner, who looked to be around fifteen years old. Phil was Mr. Macho and quite a ladies' man. We would go to the local villages and bring back some local ladies to party with and invited the whole camp. That also made us the most popular GIs in the area.

One time we went into a village and were tanked up a bit. We had always been told to stay away from back streets and to stay close to home, but we were feeling invincible. When we entered an old hut, feeling bullet-proofed, I told the guys to stay alert because I just sensed that something wasn't right. We were met by three gorgeous looking French-Asian women who wanted to party for a price. We bartered with them and were led into a room with couches and beds. I whispered to the guys to keep a weapon nearby just in case, and they looked at me like I was crazy.

I had my Luger tucked in the back of my pants. As we began with the women, I looked into a window, which reflected back, and I saw a shiny metal object coming from behind the pillow of the woman I was with. It was a ten-inch knife ready to be plunged into my backside. I whipped out the Lugar and put it to her head. She dropped the knife. I shouted a warning to the other men. They also found hidden weapons under the pillows and cushions where they had been lying.

We shot up, looking for enemy soldiers who might have been hiding in ambush positions. Finding none, we nonetheless gutted the hooch, looking for other signs of trouble. The girls thought that we'd put a bullet in their respective heads for sure, but we knew they were merely following Vietcong orders, and we just wanted to get out of there.

A factor also was that we were not supposed to be in that part of town and didn't want the authorities to know we had been there. We hightailed it out of there, thankful to get back to camp alive.

That was our last trip downtown to that area.

CHAPTER 20
IT'S BLACK AND WHITE

Being in a new locale, I had hoped that the tensions between black and white soldiers may have simmered down, or supposed the tension was just an anomaly within the two areas of the country where I had already served. In fact, the gulf between the two was a chasm. In a war where we really needed each other to survive, the racial divide was huge. There were two wars going on all the time, that is, the Vietnam War and the racial war, which seemed to be covered up by the brass.

In this third assignment, I saw fights breaking out all over the base and environs. In the field, it was not uncommon for rifle fire to be aimed at somebody not the enemy. Long Binh was an uneasy place to be in, and one was never quite sure how to handle situations.

I gradually learned that there in the rear base of Long Binh, racism, a two-way street, reared up frequently because there was more exposure to the news about the civil rights movement back in the states. I tried to keep my nose clean, but the gangs of whites beating up blacks and vice versa continued unabated. I hated the thought that I was spending more time fixing wounds inflicted by one American to another.

One day, I was in the commissary to pick up some toothpaste and other personal supplies. I heard yells and screams from behind the hooches about two hundred yards away.

As I approached the area, I saw about twenty African American soldiers beating two white GIs. The white soldiers were bleeding copiously, and it looked like they would be killed by their black brothers-in-arms.

I didn't know what to do since I was alone and was looking around for help.

All of a sudden, black Sgt. Maj. Stanton Hawkins came upon the scene. I didn't know how he'd handle the situation. I was ashamed that I even thought he might help his brothers inflict more injury.

Major Hawkins had a stentorian tone. He jumped into the fray, shouting orders to cease fighting. The men listened to him. He had averted a dangerous situation. I regarded him as a real hero.

I wish this had been an isolated situation. Instead, fights popped up all over camp, instigated as much by white GIs as any minority-fueled fight.

I and others were now receiving more information about the civil rights struggle back in the states since we had more access to the news. The Civil Rights Act of 1964 and the Voting Rights Act of 1965 did little to help. Segregation continued despite the laws.

Malcolm X (assassinated in 1965) and Fred Hampton, who was a Black Panther killed by the police in 1969, all became martyrs to the cause. The grand jury looking into the slaying of Mr. Hampton had rejected the self-defense argument tendered by the police, yet nobody was indicted. When Angela Davis was put on by Edgar Hoover in the FBI's most wanted list in 1970, racial tension flared up. Her capture in October 1970 set off riots on some bases and a lot of fisticuffs here.

I was aware that the Southern Christian Leadership Conference (SNCC) had opposed the Vietnam War as far back as 1966. I could not hope but wonder whether the black soldiers felt they were again enslaved because of the draft which cherry-picked their youth who, because of poverty, couldn't even attend colleges. So they were prime targets to be recruited and killed on foreign soil.

What was puzzling to me was the fact that white soldiers seemed to have more respect for foreign soldiers, who were assisting us in battle. There was a tribe of Koreans from the Republic of Korea (ROKS) who fought on our side and had no fear of dying for the cause. They were fierce fighters and the last to leave the scene, which was admirable. Yet many black soldiers had done exactly the same thing but were not appreciated for their valiant fighting.

There was also a tribe of Montagnards (French for mountain people), who were important allies. The Montagnards were not Vietnamese but Polynesian. They were instrumental in helping us launch offensives by letting us know enemy locations and movements. They had no love for the Vietcong or North Vietnamese. They were spiritual people who lived off the land and treated you like brothers as long as you did the same.

One time, a scout told us that there were badly injured GIs including some dead. I, and another medic, went to the scene and found two GIs decapitated. I inquired as to what happened. Those GIs had come into the Montagnard's camp area and forced themselves on a couple of women there. Ironically, the elders would give a soldier a woman if they liked you and you showed respect for their culture, but you were never, ever, to show disrespect by taking a woman by force. These soldiers would be reported as KIA (killed in action). Yet even though brother GIs had been slain and others would also be killed for the same infraction, there appeared to be more respect for that tribe than for a fellow American.

I was just perplexed at the amount of animosity on both sides that raged in that base.

CHAPTER 21

THE LAST LAP

I would soon be entering my last lap. My duties had taken on a new role, namely to find the cause of diseases that were popping up and to solve related medical problems in connection to Vietnam's climate and the war.

The medics had gotten word that many local villages outside our perimeter were having an epidemic of severe poisoning. I was part of a team who went out to investigate the problem. Hundreds were deeply sick and many had already died from this unknown new killer was. Of course, the concern also was that it would reach the base.

Days went by, and we couldn't get a handle on what was killing the people. One of our lab workers, Simon Brady, noticed a young village child drinking from a local well that was fed with water from a stream. The child seemed to have an immediate cough and respiratory difficulty. Brady followed the stream and found that the Vietcong were placing decomposing bodies into the water to poison the villagers they perceived were friendly to Americans. Brady became a hero to many by locating and stopping this version of biowarfare.

I received a notice that I would get a weekend R & R pass to Vũng Tàu. I really needed a break. I was being revisited by nightmares and spiritual visions at night. I had a recurrent dream of seeing people in various stages of need. Some had body parts missing, some were blind, others were starving, and some were just looking for the milk of human kindness to ease their tortured souls.

Just before the vacation, John, Phil, and I, with the help of local villagers, started to construct our own hooch. When completed, we decked it all over with peace symbols and graffiti, and it became the meeting and party place for many guys. Because of my combat experience, I was looked up to and I became somewhat of the social director.

One night during a get-together, we heard loud gunshots seeming to come from next door. We rushed out, and there on the ground were two GIs, one crying and the other lying with a mortal wound to his head. Both men were all drugged out and had been playing Russian roulette. One of them was unlucky.

Here was another unnecessary casualty of war. Looking at this big waste of a life started my twitching all over again. I was ruminating about how this man's family would be told that his cause of death was combat related. I wondered about whether numbers were kept for those who truly bought the farm on the field versus those who died form their own negligence. From my experience I felt the ratio was fifty to fifty.

Lying down on my cart that night, I couldn't wait for Phil, John, and me to go to Vũng Tàu.

For me, this was the best destination for relaxation. There were an estimated one hundred bars, many bearing the name of US towns or familiar places. It was the best place also to score a little companionship. I still had to be careful there since it was rumored that the Vietcong also took holidays there. The guy drinking next to you at a watering hole might be the enemy. We had MPs patrolling the place though, so it was relatively safe.

While we three musketeers were there, we met every pothead and wheeler-dealer in existence. I stuck to 3.2 beers and watched the surf crash on the sand in order to get my head cleared out. Vietnam was a beautiful place with majestic mountains and lush vegetation, and when I let my mind wander a bit, I felt that I was back at home in Narragansett, Rhode Island. If the war had not happened, this would have been a first class tourist place.

John and Phil liked to partake of a little weed or two, so for that trip, they were blown away. I still did not take dope. At a show, I met a gorgeous gal, and I spent beaucoup bucks on her, taking her to a wonderful nightclub show. We went back to my hotel room. When I woke up in the morning, all the money was missing from my wallet.

I borrowed some money from Phil for the next day's activities. They again went for weed, and I for other earthly entertainment. I led them home again, and when we were ready to get a good night's sleep, John crawled into bed only to find that a snake had already hit his sack. It plunged its teeth into his left leg. John chopped off the snake's head with a twelve-inch machete and screamed for help.

Phil and I led him to an infirmary. We carried the dead snake so the doctor would know what venom had gone into him. It turned out to be a very poisonous specimen, and he was lucky that the got to the infirmary in time.

The party was now officially over for the weekend, and we packed to get back to base camp the next day. Before we left, we were visited by a couple of con artists who wanted us to go to an underground bunker that was filled with ladies of the night and a lot of drugs to keep New York City high for a month. Remembering our last experience with unknown ladies off the beaten path, we passed it up.

Several weeks later, we learned that government officials had cleaned out this very bunker and some court marshals were underway.

The last thing I needed was to be thrown out of the service with such a short time left. Court marshals follow you forever.

"The Spray That Keeps on Killing"
Agent orange spraying which caused severe
problems for GI's some, resulting in death.

CHAPTER 22

SHORT-TIMER

By now I had served ten months in the country and was about to become a short-timer. A short-timer was given the best jobs and basically the run of the camp. The commanding officer first gave me the job of spraying from helicopters. I was told that I'd be ridding the areas of mosquitoes, which were causing malaria among the troops. I considered that a noble calling.

During the Vietnam War, the air force was usually in charge of aerial spraying missions over South Vietnam. The operation was known as Ranch Hand. The idea was to defoliate jungle areas and deprive the communists of cover. The other motive was to destroy the crops, which would sustain the enemy. The Ranch Hand motto, Only We Can Prevent Forests, was a play on the Smokey Bear injunction at the time, "Only you can prevent forest fires".

The various herbicides used each had a name of a color, such as Agent Purple, Black, White, Orange, Blue, or Pink. The UH-1 Huey helicopter was used for the mosquito spraying.

A few times a day, usually in the early morning because the rising heat of the day could cause the vaporized chemicals to float up instead of drift down, I would climb into a 'copter where there would be a large barrel of a chemical clamped to the floor. A hose ran from the barrel, and a nozzle was adapted to spraying a large area. We could wear overalls if we wanted to, but there was no protective gear for one's upper body nor was there any face masks or arm coverings. Since it was very hot in Vietnam, I declined the overalls.

I then commenced my trips with the warrant officer Tony, who manned the chopper, which would barely clear the trees. I was not air force, and I didn't know if he was, but he was my partner. The lower the spray was applied, the more effective it was supposed to be. This invited ground fire from the land below.

The smell of the chemical was putrid, particularly when it would blow back into the cockpit, which it did very frequently because of the gusts and the wind created from the helicopter blades. These trips were undertaken two to three times a day unless it was raining, which it some-times did. After close to twenty trips, I developed an extreme rash which was itchy, raw and red, and painful. My skin would sometime peel and my whole body ultimately got covered with a rash. I was checked into the MASH unit for close to two weeks and plied with prednisone and crèmes on my skin. It never quite cleared up.

Over the years, this rash would plague me. Even now, I have prob-lems with this rash. In 2013, I was on prednisone, 20 mg. a day from February to June, for some 140 days. I had to use an astringent solution called Domeboro. Each and every year, I have had recurring bouts of this rash for many weeks at a time, particularly when it is humid out.

I've checked into the veteran's hospital quite a few times for treat-ment. They attempted to get my medical records from the Long Binh MASH unit hospital, but it disappeared. I will never know for certain if I was spraying Agent Orange unawares, but I had noticed that on a couple of trips, the 'copter had passed over an area where I had previously sprayed, and the forest was denuded. I am told now that nobody knew what was in the barrel I was spraying.

I never then or now received compensation for this skin disorder. When I visited VA hospitals, as much as the burning sensation would sometimes drive me crazy, I'd see other veterans with missing limbs and blank looks, so I considered myself lucky that I still had my body intact and my facilities fairly sharp.

After getting out of the hospital, my last assignment turned out to be kind of bizarre. I was told that I'd be in charge of the day workers who filled sandbags at the base every day. There was a deeper reason why we had these workers and why they were all women. Every morning, I would drive a truck to the nearby village to pick up about twenty-five "workers". The first day, the sergeant in charge accompanied me. He walked me through the process of choosing the young ladies. They would have to be comely, and I would I'd sometimes have to direct them to the showers if they had any dirt on them. I also would have to give them blood tests to make sure they were clean. We needed to conserve the penicillin on the base.

On any given day, about half of them would fill the sandbags while the other tended to the soldier's needs. Then there would be a reverse rotation. All in all, about two hundred girls were involved in this program.

Each day, when I would arrive at camp with the ladies, the guys would line up to see whom I brought. They would all have their favorites, and I went out of my way to provide a variety of talent.

As I subsequently learned, there were other "pimps" like me from other units, also driving the day workers to and from the camp for each respective unit. The men would pay me about $6, of which $2 would be paid to the girl per trick, $2 for me, and $2 for the master sergeant for each encounter. We rationalized that these trips were necessary to cut down the men's need to leave the base to go into town. In the past, some soldiers had either gotten shot or came down with a nasty disease.

I certainly was not only popular with the men but also with the ladies, who vied with each other to earn money at the camp. Many of these young women were so beautiful, they could have been movie stars in another life. With poverty lurking on every corner, the families encouraged this commerce.

About once a week, a bus would leave to go to Saigon, and I'd be on it. It was like Mardi Gras every time we got there. Most of the young ladies by then knew me by name. I remember one night when I delivered girls in shopping carts to GIs as part of our version of room service.

It wasn't until after I left Vietnam that I realized what a derelict I had become. I didn't even see the disconnect between those wild outings and the fact that thousands of other GIs were being wounded for life or killed in the country.

I still wasn't a happy camper when I was alone. I continued to shake and twitch. Helicopters heading in my direction would make me conjure up the dead and maimed bodies. I just couldn't shake the horrible images.

As my time grew short in the country, I began to dream about going back home. It was sort of an idealized longing since the country had changed quite radically, and many Americans hated our guts. Finally, I received my orders to go home, and although I was excited, I really didn't know what I was going to do when I get there. I had no degree, my head was really messed up something bad, and the world had changed drastically.

Sarge called me and told me to pick my replacement for the day worker job. Up to that point, I should have been going home with thousands of dollars, but I blew it on wine and women but no song. I decided that I could have a stash by selling this job, which I had gotten for the bubble. I took bids. Joe Anziloni from New York City outbid everyone, and I was $1,500 richer. He was a good businessman, so I know I was turning it over to somebody who could do the job.

I had felt like a rock star with the girls calling me Honcho, a name of respect during my procurement of the live bodies' stint. The moment Joe took over, the girls acted like they never had seen me in their lives. Everything was now Joe.

The day finally came, and I said my good-byes to my brethren. My adventures were just about to begin, and my life would change many times over for the next seven years.

CHAPTER 23

HEADING HOME

I had mixed feelings about my orders that shipped me out of Vietnam. I would be in a holding company at the Bien Hoa Air Base and processed there for transfer to the United States. I'd get to go home for at least a couple of weeks before being sent to a fort somewhere in the USA to finish up my remaining eight months of my hitch. On the one hand, I was excited to go home, but on the other, I thought I was returning with an empty sack. I hadn't achieved a college degree, my head was messed up something bad, and from what I could tell, the world had changed drastically while I was away.

At Bien Hoa, they confiscated everything that wasn't military issue. I kissed good-bye to my two pearl-handled pistols and the German Luger, all of which I hated giving up. They also cut off my long hair. I again had a shaved head, so everybody could guess that I was a soldier when I returned. I was consulted about what station I would like, and I said Fort Devens, Massachusetts, or Fort Dix, New Jersey, since either would be near my home in Rhode Island. I would get my orders in about a week.

I had some trepidation as I boarded the plane, which would take me to the base in California as the next stop to my eventual return to see my family. Other soldiers on the plane were warning about an inhospitable reception. A few verbal arguments broke out en route as GIs debated the merits of our involvement in Vietnam. A few had become doves while others were hawks. I was neither. I was just a soldier who wanted to get home in one piece.

I landed with a few dollars in my pocket from my deal with Joe Anziloni and with about half of my brain. As I got off the plane, we were met with protests and bombarded with garbage and tomatoes. Looking at the protest participants who had long hair and funny clothes, I thought that we must have headed south to Mars instead. I quickly concluded that I'd never fit in and recalculated whether I should have reenlisted.

I hopped on another plane and landed in Boston's Logan Airport where my family was waiting for me. The reunion touched my heart. I really felt myself choke up as I hugged my dad and my mother, who were obviously happy to see me alive. My ever-loving supportive sister squeezed the lifeblood out of me as she gave me a half-Nelson hug. We made small talk in the car as we drove south to Rhode Island. I started to see, by some of the comments they were making, about "ungrateful college students who didn't realize the sacrifices that soldiers were making for their country," that it wasn't going to be easy to acclimate myself to this new society.

In fact, at my family home in Cranston, I acted like I was in cloister. I didn't go anywhere. When I saw protests on TV, I shut it off. My head was still spinning with the images of Vietnam and the limbless Specialist Marshall revisited my dreams. I would shudder if I heard a plane or helicopter overhead flying in or out of TF Green airport since my home was on one of the flight paths. God forbid that a car should backfire and remind me of the firefights I had been in.

After about a week, I got a call from two of my longtime friends, Tom and Dwight, who talked me into going downtown. I half-wondered if my parents had called them to get me out of the house. I was anxious about this first excursion since my ball-e-bean haircut hadn't grown out, and even in civvies, I looked like a GI from central casting.

Tom and Dwight picked me up, and I noticed that they were wearing the fashionable clothes while I had only my duds from college that hung on me from the weight I lost. I looked like the geek of the week.

My pals ignored my clothes and didn't comment about how I looked since they didn't want me to feel awkward. Off we went to club.

I held up the walls of every establishment we visited that night, so awkward and feeling out of place was I. Tom and Dwight knew everybody in the saloons and were having a hell of a time while I was getting dirty looks from the coeds and couldn't even attract the bowwows. I went home feeling emptier and concerned that I'd never fit in again.

A couple of days later, Dwight fixed me up with a date. I reluctantly accepted it since I knew she was only doing it as a favor to Big D. When we met, she didn't even look me straight in the eyes and addressed her hello to my right shoulder. We went off to a hotspot in Boston, and she sat against the window and ignored me for the entire evening. She was monosyllabic when she answered me. Several guys in the place who obviously hated Vietnam vets stared at me and mouthed obscenities and flipped me the bird. I wanted to punch them out. My adrenaline was flowing fast, and I could have decimated them but I fumed in silence. My date made no effort to convey anything other than her contempt of being with a warmonger.

Dwight felt sorry for me, but it wasn't his fault, and he was only trying to get me to fit in. On the way home, he brought up wanting to stop at a local watering hole for last call, but she demanded to be taken home. When we pulled up to her house, she bolted out of the car without as much as a good night.

I spent the next few days in a cocoon of my own making since I was afraid of going anywhere because of the antiwar sentiment and the fact that my anger management over this treatment wasn't the best. In fact, I began to be happy that I'd be returning back to the military very soon.

When I peeled open the envelope with my orders, I expected to see one of my choices. I reread the notice again. I was heading to Fort Ord in Monterey on the opposite coast from my home. I didn't know whether to laugh or cry. I had five days to report, so my buddies took me to Cape Cod, Massachusetts, for my final weekend. We became habitué's of a bar called On the Rocks. I took my position holding up the wall again when, all of a sudden, the most beautiful girl I had seen in a long time started our way. Tom and Dwight began to bet on which one of them she wanted. And both were ready to go in for the kill. I turned away, so they could compete for her company. She tapped me on the shoulder, and when I turned around, she asked me to dance. The guys' jaws were agape.

I meekly went on to the dance floor. All eyes in the place seemed to be on this ravishing beauty dancing with a GI geek. She told me that her brother was in the service and that she was unhappy about how he had been treated while on leave in the homeland. I felt really good that somebody cared, and we danced the night away. I would never see her again, but she gave me some confidence along with a determination that I needed to go on with my life. She was a godsend that evening.

CHAPTER 24

CALIFORNIA OR BUST

There are harder things in life than being in the Monterey area of California. Fort Ord also wasn't the worst place to spend my last month's serving Uncle Sam. I reported for duty and met my new bunkmate, John Downey. I could tell practically immediately that he was from Brooklyn, New York, with his accent. Unfortunately, he was the bunkmate from hell. He was addicted to all sorts of drugs, and he was mainlining heroin. Every day, I had to watch him shoot up into nonexistent veins all over his body. Every inch of him was covered black and blues from needles, including his fingers or toes or anyplace where he'd try to find a vein. He wanted me to join his little heroin club so that there would be more money available to put in to a buy.

One night when I was sound asleep, I woke up to find him trying to shoot me up with some juice. He thought he could get me addicted, and I would be trapped like him. I almost put them through the wall and promised that he would never see another sunrise if he came near me again.

The very next morning, I asked for a transfer to another barrack and settled in with another druggy, but at least this one stayed on his side of the room. It seemed like I constantly had come into contact with every user in the army, and now I had to survive another war with drugs.

Another big problem at the fort was the continuing racial saga. Whites and blacks were rarely seen mingling together. There was always tension at the fort. I met great African Americans on a one-on-one basis, but in a group, you had to stay away or else a fight would ensue. Fights on this base were as common as the California sunshine.

I stayed away from the hassles and even dated a few "soul sisters" as the parlance of the time call them. I must say that the women didn't seem to be into the struggle as much as the men. They were wonderful to talk to, and they could give insights into the racial divide without engaging in combat. I learned a lot from these women.

There was one club in town, which was frequented by actresses and models, and every night, I tried to score unsuccessfully. All the foxes were either looking for directors or producers to further their respective careers. Occasionally, they would abandon the notion of fame and end up with a wealthy businessman instead and settle down. I plotted on how I was going to break down the barriers in that club.

I hatched a deal with a fellow GI at the Club Monterey, which would change my life in California and make me a hero at large. It would cause me a week's pay, but the scheme was worth its weight in gold. I started a conversation with Alana, one of the most popular girls at the club. She was an aspiring actress, who seemed to know everyone in this upscale watering hole. I introduced myself to her and noticed that she was bored stiff, standing and talking to a nobody soldier and was about to cut me off at the knees when my shill came over and interrupted our little talk.

"Are you Dr. Neil Richardson?" he asked on cue.

I whispered yes.

He went on with his prepared speech. "Doc, you saved my best buddy's leg from being amputated, and I cannot thank you enough. I thought this might have been you since I saw your picture in the *New York Times*."

He went on to note that I was the first celebrity he had ever met. "May I have your autograph?"

I scribbled a signature on a cocktail napkin, and he went on to thank me for taking the time to speak to him. I nodded modestly.

All of a sudden, Alana's bored eyes were wide open, and she stepped closer to me to continue our conversation.

"So you are a surgeon at the base?"

I replied yes and asked her not to tell anyone because some of the operations I was performing were still in the final testing stages. But somehow I knew that she'd be bragging to the whole place that she had met the "famous Dr. Richardson."

From that day on, I never bought another drink in that place, and life was about to become a lot easier to take. I didn't want any part of my real self, and being somebody else gave me real confidence.

Every night when I went to the club, people would shout out, "Hi, Doc! How you doing?" and introduce me to family, friends, and business colleagues.

Alana kept very close to me and did not want to share me with any other girls. From time to time, I would get a request to look at or discuss an ailment. Because of my experience as a medic, I had accumulated a wealth of knowledge, and I always came up with good advice.

Several weeks into the sham, Alana asked me to move in with her and her six-year-old daughter. I had told her that I had plans to set up a practice in San Diego, so she started to have dreams of being a doctor's wife. Her pad was a lot better than the barracks at Fort Ord, so I accepted the invite to live there on weekends. Eventually, she bought me a secondhand car to drive myself back and forth to her place.

But now, I had to make sure that she couldn't find out who I really was in Fort Ord, so I had to cover my tracks. I asked the WACS, who were the receptionists at the base hospital, to help me out. If she called to talk, they would tell her that I was in surgery and that I would call back. It worked like a charm, and she thought that I was the most in demand person that she knew. My real job at the base was helping out with special services and giving VD shots at the clinic.

One time, I had a close call with her. Before she bought me the car, she dropped me off at the officer's side of the base. She waved good-bye and stayed there until I disappeared from view. I checked to make sure she had gone and then hightailed it over to the noncom's barracks.

But time was going to catch up with me.

CHAPTER 25
A DAY OF RECKONING

I was the apple of Alana's eyes but would shortly become its rotten core. During the good times, she catered to my every whim. I mentioned that she had bought me a shiny red car with flower decals on it, but she also purchased all sorts of stylish clothes and gifts for me. I started to feel a pang of conscience. It was wonderful being Dr. Neil Richardson and not dealing with me but I was feeling dread that I would end up hurting her along the way.

One weekend when I arrived at her home, she had visitors waiting to meet me. She had flown her mother and father in from Tennessee, and they were excited to meet their daughter's main man, a notable doctor. I sat there and continued to weave the lie about setting up my practice in California and running a clinic for people with special needs. I sounded like Dr. Albert Schweitzer. They were deeply impressed with my cock-and-bull story and left, falsely assuming that their daughter would be taken care of for life. Alana was thrilled that her parents liked me and I knew this charade was getting out of control.

The next day, I went to the base hospital to put in my hours when four of my fellow medics cornered me. They had found out about my con, and now they wanted in on it, or they would blow my cover. Their proposition was for me to have Alana fix each of them up with her actress friends and they would start their own scams pretending to be doctors.

"This should be easy for you," one of them said. "You can introduce us as your colleagues from the hospital, which, in a way, we are."

I had one of the WACS who had a crush on me put together false identification cards for these guys. The IDs stated that they were MDs. Most of Alana's friends were starving actresses, and having a professional man on their arms would be a welcomed situation. And so it was that the doctors of radiation technology, oncology, pathology, and gynecology were all properly introduced, and I wondered how I was going to get out of this situation in one piece. It was getting harder and harder for me to make the masquerade work. Alana was putting a lot of pressure on me to make a decision about our relationship.

The truth was I was seeing some WACs on the side, including the one who made the phony IDs. I really had no intention of being a one-woman man. I begged off on any commitment and put off decisions to become permanent by telling Alana I had to attend a medical conference for a few days, and I headed down the coast to Carmel to clear my head.

At a club, I met a young lady who took me to a party at her house. She neglected to tell me that it was a drug and orgy party. I looked around at all the nude bodies running around and the abundance of drugs everywhere. I headed out the back door. I obviously didn't mind looking at the beautiful forms of the women, but the drugs turned me off completely.

In Carmel, I attended a party by one of my all-time favorite matinée idols, Kim Novak. She was still quite striking in 1970, but not what I saw up on the silver screen. This actress to the world was just another person caught up in the Hollywood fantasy land and bright lights. I thought how ironic that I would have such a thought since I was in another world too and needed to get off the merry-go-round.

What I was going to do with Alana and her plans to be Mrs. Dr. Neil Richardson's wife quickly unfolded beyond my control. Upon my return to the base, I received my release from active duty and my tickets to fly home to Rhode Island. Like a true coward, I could not face confessing my lies and deceit. Just as a thief in the night, I flew home without ever telling her the truth.

I felt bad on one level, but I hate confrontation. This was another facet of my chameleonlike personality. I often wondered later what happened to her and hoped that she met somebody who was sincere since she shouldn't be saddled with a loser like me at that point in her life.

My troubles, however, were about to take another turn as I headed home.

CHAPTER 26
A DOSE OF REALITY

As I stepped off the plane in Rhode Island, my supportive family was there to greet me. On my way home, my father quickly turned to the business at hand.

"What are your plans?"

"I dunno," I responded.

"Well, Jimmy, you gotta get your ass in gear. Go back to school and get your degree."

He just didn't understand that I was a far different person than the lad who left for the army. I had to get my head cleared. My nights were filled with nightmares of mangled bodies and homeless Asian or Asian American children. Pictures of hands reaching out for help dominated my dreams. My twitch became apparent as the aircraft flew over the yard, and I would duck my head to get away from the memories. I guess I had a touch of post-war syndrome but I was too proud to seek help for that.

My first week back my body broke out with the rashes that would burn, itch and break open into open sores. Weeks would elapse before I healed. The VA would douse me in solutions and medication. I was a prisoner in my own body. The doctors couldn't tell me if I had been exposed to Agent Orange or other nasty chemicals.

I couldn't do the simplest task and could not leave the house. After much effort, I decided to take my father's advice and applied to Roger Williams University in order to finish up my degree. Thank god for the

GI Bill. I tried to pay attention to my studies and to forget my problems, particularly my nightmares. School now came easier to me, and I finished my studies cum laude in business. I was feeling like a leper though, and I avoided people when I was in full bloom from the breakouts.

I went out to find a job, which pleased my dad since I had lived off him for a year.

Regrettably, during the next six years or so, I couldn't hold down a job. I was a hell of a grill man at McDonald's because I could cook dozens of hamburgers without burning any. I'd show up chronically late and get canned. I'd be taken back because of my culinary skills then get fired again. I went to work for a manufacturer in my state that made the lipstick-size cases for ChapStick. When my rashes episodically returned, I got fired again. It just wasn't my hands; it was my head. I went from job to job, hating all of them.

I acclimated initially to a job at Jane Brown Hospital, which a fraternity buddy had helped me land. Although the job was boring and a dead end as far as career was concerned, I met some very interesting people at the hospital. I befriended many nurses and doctors, and at a drop of a hat, I was off to party with them. One of the nice experiences was the annual talent show that I engineered for the staff, and it was a big hit. The girl that Dwight had fixed me up with happened to be in the audience that night. She saw me there and at a few clubs where I performed. I must have looked very different because she didn't recognize me, but I surely remembered her. She came up to me during a break and asked me if I was with anyone. I replied in the negative. I then told her that I knew somebody who had gone out with her, and she asked who it was.

"Jim Squadrito."

"That loser. Talk about somebody who didn't have a clue what to do on a date."

I then told her that some people said I looked like him.

"No way," she responded.

I then showed her my military identification with my name on it. She sheepishly stared at it and walked away. We'd never speak to one another again, not that I cared.

I did intake at the hospital. Of course, I wasn't doing any of the healing, so I felt useless as a desk jockey, and I quit when a doctor told me about another position at Blue Cross. He was a doctor in good standing with them.

So I went to Blue Cross. Initially, I was hired because I had been a medic, so I looked forward to processing claims, using my medical knowledge at a whopping $8,000 per year. Instead, I got assigned to screening cases in order to deny claims on the basis that the services performed were actually plastic surgery, which wasn't covered by medical insurance. Believe me, I got many a bribe to process cases that were primarily plastic surgery, but I turned them down. This job had a career path, but my nightmares would dog me. I gradually became disgusted, however, on being a no man to claims, but I put up with it since I could see a light at the end of the tunnel with a promotion imminent.

But I made a fatal mistake. I am an inveterate pleaser, so I sought acceptance and tried to entertain everyone, including some of the bosses. All aspiring executives like me, however, were not supposed to be fraternizing with department employees. I had a need to make sure I charmed everybody in the building since it made me forget my past, and I had a lot of friends whose camaraderie I cherished. Just as I started my third year, I was summoned upstairs. Thinking that I was going to be promoted, I instead was asked to leave quietly for violating the no-fraternization rule.

A pal of mine who had a band came to my rescue, so I was back to singing in lounges and drinking and partying my life away. I labored for a time in smoke-filled lounges. I became a prisoner to the night.

I decided to be a professional party giver. I met a lot of people through entertaining and had a knack for organizing events. I had high hopes that this would give me beaucoup bucks and girls at the same time.

My partner, Steve, helped me to organize my plan of attack. I would make elaborate invitations to be given out only to the best-looking girls at various nightspots. Saturday parties were always the best because most guys were afraid to ask beauties out lest they be rejected. I could always get guys to attend since they knew that the cream of the crop of womanhood would be attending these "prestigious" gatherings.

The program worked to perfection. I would rent a large hall and charge $5.00 a head to get in, and I advertised an open bar. This open bar was a bit disingenuous since there would only be one barkeep with five hundred people in attendance, so the drinks were few and far between. I outsmarted myself because the regulars would soon bring their own booze. Still, I made money on the cover charge. The parties thrown by Big J Productions soon became known as *the* place to be if you were the in crowd.

Each month, I have one at various locations and come away with several thousand dollars at the bigger venues and always would come away with a fox on each arm.

Then one day my empire fell down. Two IRS agents undercover came to one of the parties and asked me what I was doing with the proceeds I was clearing. I was wary and didn't offer too much info. Soon I was under investigation. It took months for me to get out of this jam, so I was out on the road again, looking for work.

Next I worked for a manufacturer of jewelry. I initiated a sort of Mary Kay cosmetics approach where wives or coeds looking for some side money could sell the jewelry for a commission and/or take jewelry as their compensation. I got bored out of my skull doing jewelry, so yes, off I went again. The fact is I could not get my head around any job in order to be successful.

I did like music, so I had a few more jobs singing with a band. At clubs though, I pretended to be somebody else. In a singing gig, I was Jimmy Velvet with the voice of velvet. I often passed as Jim Fregosi, a famous baseball player at the time. Like my days with Alana, I would sit at a bar for a drink. My buddy would say to a group of girls, "Isn't that the famous singer Jimmy Velvet?" or "By god, I think that's the famous baseball star, Jim Fregosi."

He'd urge them to stay put while he'd try to persuade me to come over to the gals which, of course, I "shyly" did after I'd scribble an autograph on a bar napkin. Like most people, the girls would fall for the sham. As the saying goes, however, you can't fool all the people all of the time. One time, a gal said that I wasn't one of my personas, which was that of a prominent lawyer that night. She announced to her sorority sisters that I was Jim Squadrito, a louse with the ladies!

I moved out of my family home at age twenty-seven amid the wails of my mother who wanted me to stay. I moved in with a buddy, named Don, who ran an apartment complex. Don was a skirt-chaser and a pothead. The place was inhabited by real losers, so I was right at home. Don gave all of us a break on the rent as long as we invited him to our parties to introduce him to girls. My former partner, Steve, also had several girls living there rent free as long as they serviced him every so often.

The owner of the complex lived in Boston, so Don would report the apartments empty, and the owner would just take the write-off without ever checking. Don would pocket the rent from the misfits like me.

Every so often, my rashes would return with a vengeance, so I'd be out of the lovemaking business for a while. Bad dreams still haunted me, so I never let anybody stay over, so afraid was I of nightmares lest I screamed.

The biggest problem in my life continued to plague me, namely, my failure to take on responsibility. I was also having difficulty earning enough scratch, so Don was nagging me for more dough.

I was about to take another tumble in life.

MAKING A MEMORY OF WAR
BUILDING THE VIETNAM VETERANS MEMORIAL

In 1971, angry Vietnam veterans gathered outside the White House gates and on the steps of Capitol Hill. Chanting and jeering, they hurled their Purple Hearts, their Bronze Stars, their awards of valor and bravery, over the White House fence and against the limestone Capitol. In a radical breach of military and social decorum, these highly decorated military men spit back their honors. They had been betrayed, lied to, and abandoned. They had had no chance to be Hollywood heroes; instead, they had fought an ugly war, survived, and lost.

"The Forgettable War"
From the Vietnam Memorial

CHAPTER 27

DOWN THE CHUTE THEN UP AGAIN

With my life, I was paddling as fast as I could and getting nowhere. Using aliases occasionally was wearing very thin as fun. I botched at least two relationships with ladies I cared about during this time because of my inability to grow up. I knew I needed to hold onto something, or I'd go crazy, or at least, crazier than I was.

Without a full-time job, money got real tight. I actually cut out coupons where I'd get two hamburgers for the price of one to feed myself. Don was getting pissed because I'd be late with my rent, particularly when he thought I was blowing money at parties. I had unemployment checks coming in but would soon have them run out.

I began to notice Vietnam vets walking the street. They had always been there, but it was only when I began to think that might be my plight did I ever even notice them as so far gone that I became depressed. I actually thought of ending my life before I became homeless. My Catholic guilt nixed that path.

One evening, I had a calming voice for a change speak to me in a dream. It told me not to worry and that everything would be all right.

I never had been a religious person per se, but I regarded myself as a spiritual person. I focused on the spirit that led me safely through Vietnam, and I surmised I had a broader purpose in life because I had been spared. I knew I had to reach another plateau in my life. I just didn't know how to do it.

Right before I got the heave-ho out of the apartment complex, a most wondrous event happened, and it came in the form of a snowstorm.

In the winter of 1978, I awoke to what would be a record snowfall in Rhode Island, colloquially called the blizzard of 1978. I was depressed, and the storm made me even more crazed since I would be housebound for probably days. I was out of money with no job prospects and experiencing waning respect from my family and friends.

I looked out the nearly frozen window of my apartment on that historic day and saw two men stuck in the snow outside. Their car, like so many others, was unable to move from its two-foot deep interment. I saw them abandoning the car and looking around, I guessed for shelter or, at least, a phone.

I yelled down from the porch and offered them the use of my phone, which was about a day away from being disconnected for lack of payment and a cup of coffee.

As they climbed up the stairs, they had an air of confidence and class, and I remember saying to myself, "Where did you go wrong in your life, Jim?"

They sat down on my ragged couch, sipped the last of my coffee, and made a few calls. We then sat and talked while the snow outside pelted the earth.

We talked about 'Nam and the effect the war had had on my life, and I couldn't believe I heard myself say that I needed a break from somebody to prove what I had and to get back into the game of life.

It seemed like a godsend when they informed me that they were both executives form a large corporation whose headquarters was in Minnesota. They were in town to bolster the sales force in East Providence.

One of them looked me in the eye. "Are you ready for a new challenge in your life?"

I could have cried with relief. "Just give me the chance."

He told me to report to the office in East Providence to be interviewed for a position in sales. I had no experience but just maybe a door was opening for me.

I would see these gentlemen again, but I would never forget the two hours of talking that we did about setting goals for my life. The executive who called to get me the interview was a vice president of the Copying Division.

Four days after the blizzard cleanup, I went to the interview, and much to my dismay, there were forty-five applicants in the waiting room. When my time finally came, I met Bill G., who was a street-smart guy, and he immediately told me I was overqualified for the position given all the schooling I had. They were looking for a hardened street guy with an aggressive attitude. I told him I couldn't be overqualified since I had done nothing in my life to prove otherwise. After about thirty minutes, I think he discovered that I needed a major break in my life and that got me a second interview with his top sales rep, David F. This man was a sharp cookie who didn't seem to like me a lot, particularly since the interview lasted only ten minutes. I figured my chances were slim to none, and I went back to my lonely existence to reflect.

I then received a call from Bill G. asking me to come back for a third interview, and I raced as fast as I could to get to the office. There were three finalists for the position. To be honest, I had no idea what the job entailed. I also didn't know what the salary was, but I wanted this job badly since I needed to be a part of something.

Bill told me that his reps thought I was overqualified for the job and asked me to sell him on my reasons for wanting an entry-level job. I told him I needed a new start and my motivation was to accomplish something, and if I had to do it from the bottom of the barrel, so be it. He admired my candor and told me he'd call the next day with an answer.

That night, I prayed and prayed that I would get the chance to be part of a team and show what I could do. Even though I had no experience in sales, I looked forward to the challenge if I was offered the position.

The next day, Bill called me and gave me the goods news that I had landed the job! I was ecstatic. He told me that I reminded him of him, that is, a self-starter who needed a break. The compensation package wasn't exactly overwhelming, but I would get $400 a month in salary and a 2 percent commission on total dollars sold. I would be selling copying machines and products related to the machines. I had high expectations when they told me that they also offered a car for work.

Off I went with renewed confidence and a reason to exist again. My self-doubt, though, made my head a bit shaky and my rash returned in spades. On the social side, I was a whack job and still partied too heavily with my friends at the beachcomber bar and other places. I slowly came to the realization though that I would have to make a change in my personal life or I would flame out. It was time to become responsible.

CHAPTER 28
NEW BEGINNINGS

Things were not going well with my new sales job. For starters, the rate of success was selling one for twenty cold calls or a 5 percent success rate. Pushing copy machines around corners and upstairs to potential customer's offices was backbreaking work.

I decided to take a low-key approach. I was friendly with the procurers at each business and would say words to the effect that I was there to serve them if they ever needed me and wanted to change copy machines. After six months of no sales I was summoned by Bill G.

"Ya don't have any sales," he told me as though I didn't know.

"I am laying the groundwork," I replied.

"Groundwork or not, kid, you have two more weeks to land a sale. Otherwise, I have to cut you loose. Sorry."

I was down. It was hard living on $400 measly dollars a month, and now I was headed out the door again. Then something happened that for me was a bona fide miracle.

I had visited AT Cross, a leading manufacturer in Rhode Island. The business had twenty-five copy machines from another company. I had had a nice conversation with their manager and thought that I had a good rapport with him.

He called me and invited me to visit him during what might have been my last week of work.

"I remember what a nice young man you were when you came here. I seem to recall that you promised also to oversee any complaints or maintenance issues personally and promptly. Was I right about that?"

"Absolutely."

"Well, I'm sick and tired of the poor service we are getting from the present company. They're lease is up. I want twenty-five copiers from your company to lease right away. Can you do that'?"

I almost fainted as I assured him that he'd never get better service from anybody as much as he would from me. I think I floated back to Bill G.

"So, kid, are you going to give up the ghost?" he asked when he saw me.

"I have twenty-five copiers going to AT Cross," I nearly shouted it with happiness.

He looked surprised and congratulated me.

I was on a roll. I always was there immediately to give service if anything happened to one of our copiers. The procurer was also the chair of a group of business managers like himself, and he would give them my card while talking about the wonderful guy I was and how the service had improved 1,000 percent. Soon I was getting orders from each of them. I shot up to be the salesperson with the most lease/purchases in the business by the end of one year. By then, my company was also doling out a 5 percent bonus for supplies, so I was raking in the money for selling duplication paper as well. I felt that I had arrived!

At night though, I was still hitting the bar circuit and ending up with some girls whose name I couldn't remember in the morning. I was popular because now I had money to spend freely, but I was dying inside. I knew I had to stop this self-destructive action, but I seemed unable to curb my excesses.

Then one day I met a girl who said her name was Janet. I thought she was coming on to me, so I figured she'd be another notch in my belt and leave it at that.

When she said she had been watching me for weeks and had wanted to meet and speak with me, I figured the rest would be history. After putting on my best moves on her, we decided to go back to my apartment. I fetched a couple of beers from the fridge. As I approached her, I saw a book in her hands.

HOLY BIBLE was stenciled on the cover. She opened the scriptures and began to read it to me. Now I was brought up Catholic, but that was ridiculous. I figured that one of my buddies or some jilted chick had put her up to doing this. Trying to block out what she was reading, I put on my best finishing moves on her. My aggressive style didn't work this time. In fact, it was her moves that would have a huge impact on me.

CHAPTER 29
TAKING A RIGHT CURVE

The young lady continued her readings from the Holy Book, all of which centered on being born again. I listened as politely as I could for close to two hours and finally said, "Let's get out of here and get something to eat." We headed for a diner that was open 24/7.

Over bacon and eggs (toast for her), she started to preach to me again about changing my lifestyle, and it suddenly dawned on me that she wasn't acting. She was thoroughly convinced that her ministry was to make me change my life.

After dining, we returned back to my pad. She continued to read biblical passages and explained what each meant. All of a sudden, I became lightheaded and felt being drawn into a vortex. I wasn't in the throes of a hangover. I certainly wasn't lightheaded because I was hungry since I had just downed a yeoman's meal.

This will sound crazy, but I saw a light that seemed to shine from nowhere, and a male voice was telling me to make a commitment to the Lord Jesus and to be born again. The light and voice penetrated into my very soul. I spoke aloud, making a commitment to change my life for the good of my soul and mankind.

I'm aware of what skeptics might think. All I can say was that I experienced a transformation at that very moment.

Janet smiled at me. We made plans to meet the next day where she'd take me to a prayer meeting where other born-again people would be there. I sat down the next morning at a church that had close to seventy-five–eighty congregants. When it was my turn to speak, I addressed the group and started with an introduction of Janet, who had brought me there. When I looked around, she was gone. I asked people if they knew her, and nobody did. I have never seen her again although I did try to find her for years. It was as though she never existed. I began to wonder if she was the figure in Vietnam, that is, my own guardian angel who had protected me for that moment of conversion.

For months, I walked around, afraid to say anything to anyone since the story sounded so nuts. With no more parties or drinking binges, my popularity began to wane. So-called friends left me one by one because I wasn't fun anymore, and they didn't want me to tell them anything about what had happened to me on the few occasions I broached the subject with folks I thought were close friends. Despite the rejection, in its place, I was happier than I ever was.

I finally told my family who, while gratified for my change in direction, nonetheless worried about me when I stayed home. I had dreams where spirits would speak to me and tell me that everything was going to be okay.

I joined a so-called born-again church where I would be fed the Word, and I started to believe in myself again. The sermons helped me to handle my new life and to find the middle road.

One night, I was visited by a spirit and told that I was chosen to help the poor and forgotten people of the world and that I would be told how. Each night, for days on end, I would find myself in my dreams in the bodies of these poor unfortunates and felt the pain that endured in their lives. One night, for example, I found myself in the body of a homeless man who lived in a cardboard box. As people passed by without even a sideways glance, I felt the pain of this forgotten man. If they had at least said hello or at least acknowledged my existence, I believe that I would have felt hope. Nobody thought to even nod their heads at me, and I wished for a quick death.

Several nights later, I dreamed that I was confined to a wheelchair and physically felt the stares of passersby, but I never heard a kind word or encouragement from any one of them to help me through the day. I experienced the depression that must be a part of all the handicapped community and why my brothers and sisters in life could not help my pain. I'd wake up in a sweat and pondered the lives of these tortured souls.

Many times during my sleep, I would be transported to homeless shelters and elderly homes to witness the loneliness that mankind had decided to forget. Visits to people ravished by war were also common occurrences.

Why was I the one to be given this tour of the lost and forgotten and somehow given the mission of letting the world know of their suffering? I felt ill-equipped since I was still in the throes of getting my own life headed in the right direction. My dreams told me that I would know what to do and the time to do it if I was only patient. I know that the experts would probably say that I was suffering from posttraumatic stress but that redemptive period was much more than that in my view.

I was now in my mid-thirties and wondering if I would ever settle down. Then I met Sarah. I was convinced that God had sent her my way to save me from my misery. It didn't quite work out that way.

CHAPTER 30
ALMOST NORMAL

Sarah and I had never been completely in love. Face it. I wasn't even sure what love was. That was as close an approximation as I thought it could be. I was convinced that I should marry her as part of the Lord's master plan for me. Originally, she had hated me because she thought I was a playboy. A mutual friend introduced us, telling her that she would not believe the transformation that I had gone through. Although she was eleven years younger than me, she seemed very understanding. I did share with her my dreams to make the world a better place, and she was in sync with this aspiration. We both wanted children, and she seemed to want the same things out of life, so we convinced each other that, indeed, this would be a marriage made in heaven. We married at St. Catherine's Roman Catholic Church.

As we started our lives together, my job started to pick up, and I became one of the top sales people for my company, 3M. I was promoted to another division where I sold static control systems. Back in those days, PC boards would crash if static from the air touched the diodes. This 3M product prevented static electricity using polonium 210, which had low radiation, probably less than what a light bulb emitted. Nuclear anything got people nervous, so I would hold the product during the presentation to corporate heads of companies. What was funny was that when my rashes episodically returned, my hands would be a red mess, and my fingers would swell and contract. There I'd be in the front of the room, barely able to grip and hold up the device while there would be snickers in the audience when I said the product didn't cause any bad side effects. I eventually came clean about my Vietnam exposure to whatever chemicals there were back then, and ironically, the sympathy for me plus the superiority of the product resulted in beaucoup bucks for 3M and for me.

After we purchased our first home in North Kingstown, we would have the children talk many times over the next few years. She seemed to shrug it off. When I married her, she had been an administrative assistant in an ad agency. The principals were now going to sell it, and she wanted to buy it. She felt that she wanted to run her old business and then, once successful, bear children.

That sounded like a plan, so we invested in the business and took out bank loans and a line of credit to pay for the buyout. Although she worked very hard, the big guys in advertising had her for lunch. The business began to fail. We owed on personal credit cards as well. We soon found ourselves in a marriage with no children or money.

I blamed myself partially for the failure. I either had no time to help her because of my sales job, but if the truth be told, I was out, engaged in a new pursuit, golf on weekends. I told her and myself that it was a way to exorcize my demons from the war, but if I'm honest, I was also escaping from the tension in the marriage.

The marriage made in heaven went to hell. Sadly, we divorced after a two-year separation when our differences couldn't be reconciled. The marriage had lasted seven years officially.

Another seven year period would await me before another serious relationship came. I sold the house in North Kingstown and went into hibernation, trying to pay off the creditors. I was amazed that even though I eventually paid back all the creditors, I was saddled for seven years with the same lousy credit rating had we filed bankruptcy.

I was now renting a condo and concentrated on my job. Thank god I was employed since the demons from my war days returned in full attack mode. I was battling depression anew because of the failed marriage and the returning thoughts of Vietnam. One particular thought that dogged me around that time was whether I had killed or maimed anyone in Vietnam. I had exchanged gunfire in order to get to wounded troops but had shot in generalized areas with both a grenade launcher and M16 rifle. I would see dead North Vietnamese soldiers but wasn't sure whose GI bullet had felled them. Then there was the haunting of unwanted children. Had I brought any of these children into the world? Had any village people or little ones been maimed by my random shooting?

Then one night, two spirits came to visit me and asked me to begin a quest. I was to start a worldwide program to help the homeless, handicapped, and elderly people of the world feel wanted and worthwhile. The grandiosity of such an undertaking escaped me since I was convinced that this was to be my calling. I woke up and went to my desk to pen words and music to a song that would be the theme. I had no training in music or lyrics, but this song asks everyone to remember that we are all brothers and sisters and to acknowledge one another in ways that give meaning to lives.

"Saying Hello" was the name of the song, and the words can be interpreted as any communication for the good of mankind. It was simply a message of not forgetting people in their personal bondage throughout the world. Upon its completion, I now wanted to start a journey to find the right vehicle to promote the program.

My first step happened while I was on vacation in Florida. I was dining at Outback Steakhouse when a young woman asked if she could sit at our table while she waited for her reservation. I was seated with several friends, but I asked her to join us. As the conversation ensued, I told her of my visions and that I wanted to present the program to prominent companies to spread the word about the plight of the afflicted. It seemed like a miracle was about to happen. She told me that she was on the board of directors for a large food chain and that they might want to look at the program. I was stunned and absolutely certain that it was fate that had her sit with us. She gave me her card and asked me to call her.

I did exactly that. She sounded like she had never heard of me. When I mentioned the plan we discussed, she told me in no uncertain terms that her company is in the business of selling hamburgers and not helping the world's problems. That prominent woman who has had several books on business on the best seller list had now given me a slanted view of big business in America. To this day, I never eat at that chain. My hopes, however, were dashed but not for long. I would try other avenues.

I decided that because of the spiritual dimension to this calling, I should discuss it with a priest so I could be guided in the right way. I got short shrift. Because I was just a regular schmuck and not a high-profile church leader (shades of Monsignor Germani came back to me), I apparently was not *allowed* to have spiritual beings visit me. I was pushed aside with the equivalent of a pat on the head and a wish for good luck.

The newspaper reporters I visited never believed me, but they loved the song.

I still have not found the correct conduit yet but still live with the mission to make this happen. Except for my job though, my life at that moment was full of ups and downs. Mostly downs.

CHAPTER 31

REDEMPTION

I continued to be an abject failure at relationships. I ran through several ones, but I just couldn't focus on them. The women uniformly found me weird since I obviously talked about religion too much, and I knew that I wasn't any fun to be with. I had this compulsive need to share with them all my inner workings no matter how casual the relationship, so no wonder that I freaked them out.

Then one evening, some twenty-three years ago, I met the love of my life. Our first meeting was pretty awful though. I was dining at the Harborside restaurant in East Greenwich with my buddies, and we were encouraging the females in the room to show off their respective butts in a butt contest. Michele came in with her girlfriend, heard my encouragement of the spectacle, and left because she didn't want to share space with a jerk.

A couple of weeks later, one of her girlfriends who knew me offered to fix her up. Michele didn't connect the name with the idiot in the restaurant, but she was still reluctant. We finally met two weeks after the incident, and she promptly refused to go out with me when she saw that I was the one egging girls on at the Harborside. Our mutual friend pushed the issue. The gal owned a daycare, and one day, when I was singing to the kids, the mutual friend called Michele and let her hear me serenading the children. She figured that I couldn't be that bad after all.

Our first date was at the Lincoln dog track. She called the mother from the ladies' room to tell her where I had taken her. The mother retorted, "Dump him right now. Good god! He's a gambler. No doubt a heavy drinker. Maybe mixed up in the mob…"

I then returned with two glasses of wine and a Coke. I didn't drink because I was too stupid on alcohol. I gave her $100 to bet on the dogs, and we had a nice time.

She eventually asked me why I had brought her to the dog track.

"It's better than dinner where the date is a disaster, and you still have to get through an entire meal on small talk while watching the clock," I said.

That answer made sense to her.

I began to see Michele frequently. Her house was just across the street, so it was very convenient. At one time though, the convenience almost broke us up. I needed a cleaning lady for my new condo, and a friend of mine recommended a gal whose services he had used before. I hired her, and she began her once-a-week job. Unbeknown to me was the fact that she was a naturalist and cleaned in the nude. I walked in on her one day when she was all in her glory. She told me that it was no big deal and that was who she was. She was not the best cleaning lady, but I was worried about hurting the friend who recommended her, so I convinced myself that I was nobody to judge another.

One day, Michele came over and saw some panties lying on the couch. She was ready to accuse me of something when I told her about Ms. Nudie. The very next day, my naturalist was fired. She was replaced by Michele's ten-year-old daughter, Chantele

Speaking of Chantele, I was terrified the first time I met her and her brother Daniel. They were still trying to accept the divorce, which happened two years earlier, and the separation from their father. Trying to break the ice, I brought with me two 3M earphones that were big items for kinds on the market at that time. The earphones would help them study without interruption, so I won points with Michele too.

Over the next months, I worked very hard at finding common ground between me and each child. Dan was small and wiry but had an inbred ability to take to all kind of sports. With my basketball background, we played at local courts and he became a fine shooter and ball handler. He would also play on other teams, but his first love grew into golf as the sport. I had connections in Rhode Island and Massachusetts, which allowed me to teach and play. I set up Danny as a caddy at the Quidnesset Country Club through a friend who was a member there. My pal, Vinny, not only taught him the ropes of being an excellent caddy but he taught him the finer points of the game. Danny thrived on it. As time went on and Danny grew into a fine young man, I offered counsel on issues that he didn't want his mother to know about. No better son of my own could I ever ask for.

Chantele was a bit more complicated. I knew that the only way for her to accept me in her life was for me to try to understand hers. I listened to her problems and tried to help her through the difficult times, particularly as a teen. Chantele had some resentment toward her father. I bent over backward with both children to make sure they would reconcile with the biological father and to respect him. I am friends now with the natural father, who has thanked me for bridging the gap that ensued after the divorce. Chantel also is a daughter I could only wish as my own.

Both are successful entrepreneurs today.

Michele and I had a thirteen-year engagement, so to speak, since she didn't want to rush into anything after her first marriage ended in divorce. Personally, I think she also needed the time to sift through my baggage. I had the easier task adjusting to our relationship. I can truly say that she is the finest human being I know. She has brought me enormous happiness. I love her two children, Chantele and Daniel, as my own. I never felt that I could ever be this happy.

My personal life was fulfilled. I also have continuing success at 3M. I was promoted to an executive position in the health and safety section of the company.

Then on September 11, 2001, I would be put to another test, and one that would be a living nightmare but also redemptive. I was en route to Bath, Maine, to train a number of employees for Bath Iron Works on how to protect themselves from toxic chemicals by using the proper respiratory equipment. My phone rang, and something told me to pick it up right then rather than answer the call at the conclusion of the presentation.

Chills came over my entire body as my national director told me of the terrorist attacks, at that time, solely in New York City. Later, there would be two other acts of terrorism. I was summoned to be part of the team to help rescuers at ground zero and to utilize the equipment that I had brought to the Bath, Maine, presentation. Some of my coworkers who lived in New York City were already on site. They had witnessed the horror of the second attack and the screams coming from the victims in the towers as these poor souls jumped.

Upon my arrival, the team settled into a makeshift command center in midtown. We set up a strategy to help all rescuers, and we were all given assigned areas. We were informed that other buildings in the city may be targets like the Empire State Building and the New York Armory, so we made contingency plans for response to these buildings if necessary. My colleague, Frank Reese, and I were assigned to the armory. Our job was to train the National Guard on how to use the respirators upon entering ground zero. When we got there, the place was filled with armed police also, and above us, helicopters hovered lest there be an attack launched.

Frank and I finished several training sessions, and the colonel asked us to accompany him to ground zero to help the guardsman already deployed there. There were already hundreds of workers overcome by toxic exposures, and they were receiving treatment in area hospitals. Frank and I were to make sure that subsequent responders would only enter the area with proper protective gear. I was transported back to my Vietnam days, and I thought that this, indeed, was a war zone. Wearing security clearance badges, we entered ground zero.

Along the way, thousands of bystanders were standing behind ropes policed by guardsmen and police, and they were cheering at the top of their lungs as rescuers and workers headed in to help in any way possible. We walked through a grey tint, and the ground was covered with debris as far as the eye could see. Local companies, businesses, and restaurants were shells of their former selves. The former great towers were scattered in splinters of concrete and steel. Simmering smoke shot out of the pit, and I swear I could see spirits of those who vanished flying heavenward into the darkened sky above.

Within hours, 3M placed four 18-wheelers all loaded with equipment around ground zero. All personnel had to go through medical tests, and we fitted them with proper respiratory equipment. Unfortunately, before our arrival, the rescuers were ill-equipped and many died of respiratory distress in the hospitals or had lifelong lung damage.

Late at night, we returned to home base in midtown. The city was empty. Broadway shows were cancelled, and the only eating establishments open were feeding the responders. The spirit of teamwork and camaraderie was outstanding.

With our medical trucks now making sure that works were at least safe with their breathing on the job, Frank and I were given a new assignment at Fresh Kills in New Jersey. Dump trucks had entered the attacked zone each day with full loads of debris. They then would head to the Hudson River and dump the contents onto barges, which would then head to Fresh Kills, a huge landfill in New Jersey. Frank and I were asked by the FBI and the NYC police to make sure that the workers at the dump were using proper equipment in dealing with the debris.

We followed as the barges crossed the Hudson into New Jersey. There were a line of trucks picking up the Twin Towers' debris and then traveling on to Fresh Kills. We passed several security stations into a landfill and climbed a huge garbage mountain to the top of the dump. From there, we were able to see the trucks unloading the towers' remains in huge piles. There to receive it were FBI and NYPD personnel, who now had the job of painfully sifting through all this rubble to find any remains of victims as well as any evidence of the crimes. To say that this team was going over everything with a fine-tooth comb would be accurate. Families who suspected that their loved ones might have been killed in the attack had given the FBI samples of hair or other potential DNA items, so they could match the remains, a task not for the weak or weary. Watching the professionalism of this group of law enforcement personnel was heartening to say the least.

Frank and I patrolled among the collectors to ensure that they had proper respirators for protection against exposure from the biological remains as well as from toxic exposure. I wiped away tears as I just imagined how I would react if my beloved Michele, her kids, my parents, and sister or other loved ones had been victims. I was so sorrowful since I knew that very little would be left of the victims, some of whom had been vaporized by the intense heat or the explosions. We left Fresh Kills, a sight I will never forget, but with a sense of pride over the professionalism of the caring men and women handling the horror.

I also underwent a catharsis. Spending those several weeks at ground zero put me back in touch with the good things I had done in Vietnam as a medic saving lives. I was no longer totally down on myself.

When I came home, I hugged my family and thought of all those victims who would be denied the opportunity to do the same.

EPILOGUE

I would like to think that I have stopped being a chameleon and am now a man of principle. Occasional voices in my sleep still urge me to do more for the world. I still see images of Sp5c. John Marshall at times when I least expect it. I intend to pursue that initial inspiration to do good, particularly in light of the sacrifices made by the John Marshalls of that war.

I have immersed myself in projects to help others. I joined Big Brothers for a time. My little brother in that organization, Jonah, is now a successful owner of a construction company. I have served on the board of directors for a school for children with special needs for over 40 years. My wife and I volunteer for food banks and soup kitchens in Florida and I am a guest auctioneer for charitable events for Breast Cancer Awareness and Women who have been Domestically Abused in our community. My God giving ability to sing and entertain is put to good use with musical events that my wife Michele and I produce and direct to put smiles on people's faces and dedicate these events to our servicemen around the world. A proud participant in veterans groups and VFW member, I strive to help our returning soldiers in their quest for a better life here at home. In my single days I had fun being "auctioned off" for Cystic Fibrosis at several of their events.

Perhaps writing this book will help in some small measure my Vietnam brothers who have felt as useless as I have on many an occasion to know that there is hope. There is redemption for them as well.

To all my fallen comrades who gave their lives in the war, I will always honor your memories. To all the innocent people on all sides of that conflict who suffered because of our inability to end that conflict far sooner than we did, I apologize for the horrors your families have suffered. To the medics of that conflict, I am honored to be among your number.

I have come full circle and have experienced almost everything, the good and the bad, in life. I have a renewed confidence and spirituality. I have a wonderful marriage.

In the last few years, I have been invited to speak at colleges and universities about job opportunities in *Fortune 500* companies. I pass out cards with what I consider the formula for success that I live by. The formula is E+P+C=F.

E is for energy, and we need to have an abundance of it to make it through the day.

P is for passion that shows our love for what we do. If we don't have passion for what we decide to do in life, we will never be successful.

C is for creativity since it brings us to a higher level in life for whatever we decide to be. Try to make whatever you do better.

F is not financial, which might occur to some. It stands for *fun*. Even if you are doing well in life, if you are not having fun doing it, then it is time to move on.

I still carry the wounds of war, but I finally have peace of mind after a long journey. May my soldier brothers have the same peace.

ABOUT THE AUTHORS

James Squadrito is a decorated medic and a successful businessman. He was honorably discharged following his service in Vietnam but suffered nightmares for many years. He gradually confronted the events during his tour that caused him unrest. His journey brought him from the brink of despair to the ultimate reintegration of his ideals after a long struggle to adjust to daily living back in the United States. He now is active in veterans groups and charities. He lectures undergraduates frequently at Bryant University and acts as a volunteer liaison with alumni groups. He is inducted in the university's Athletics Hall of Fame.

Arlene Violet was the first woman elected to the position of state attorney general in the United States. Her books include Convictions, My Journey from the Convent to the Courtroom, and The Mob and Me. She was the book writer for the musical, The Family, A Mob Musical Drama. She has been the recipient of over fifty public service awards. Arlene has been a weekly columnist since 1997, a repeat panelist on a local CBS TV program, Newsmakers, and on PBS, The Lively Experiment. Arlene was a talk show host for almost twenty years. She continues to practice public interest law.